The psalms are known as the heart of the Old Te... heart of the Book of Psalms is found in this selection, which is presented at the heart of a life of peacemaking, in the heartbeat of a peacemaker. Here we see John in contemplation and action, drawing from a rich source of strength and inspiration for us all.

BROTHER PAUL QUENON, *Abbey of Gethsemani, author of* **In Praise** *of the Useless Life: A Monk's Memoir and Amounting to Nothing: Poems*

Praise Be Peace is more than a book. It is a sacred space inviting us to encounter the God of peace, stirring our deepest longings for the fullness of life and calling us to follow in the footsteps of the nonviolent Jesus. Alive with the vivifying power of the nonviolent psalms, this volume is a portable hermitage where we can be nourished to venture forth as spiritually grounded peacemakers in our wounded world.

KEN BUTIGAN, *author of* **Nonviolent Lives** *and* **Pilgrimage** **Through a Burning World**

When you look at life through the prism of Dear's spirituality, you see everything differently, ensuring that peace in all aspects of your day becomes the bedrock of your life. In the extreme violent times in which we live, John Dear's life-affirming message is both inspirational and essential, because peace and nonviolence begin within you. Like the psalms themselves, this is a book to be prayed not just read.

GERARD THOMAS STRAUB, *filmmaker and author of* **The Loneliness** *and Longing of St. Francis*

To Dennis & Tensie —

JOHN DEAR

With blessings of peace,

John

PRAISE BE
Peace

Psalms of Peace and
Nonviolence in a Time of
War and Climate Change

**TWENTY-THIRD
PUBLICATIONS**
twentythirdpublications.com

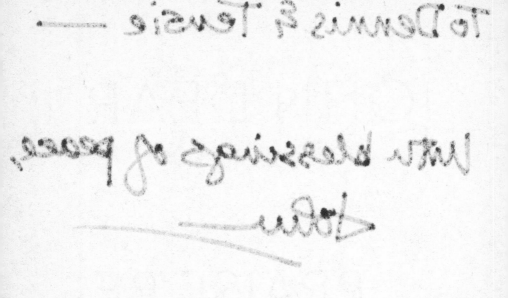

TWENTY-THIRD PUBLICATIONS
One Montauk Avenue, Suite 200
New London, CT 06320
(860) 437-3012 or (800) 321-0411
www.twentythirdpublications.com

Cover art: "Cypress by the Bay" © Fr. Arthur Poulin (http://www.fatherarthurpoulin.org)

ISBN: 978-1-62785-433-7
Printed in the U.S.A.

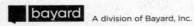

bayard   A division of Bayard, Inc.

For Ethel,
Friend and Peacemaker

Contents

III. The Beauty of Peace: The Celebration of the Peacemaker

IV. Taking Refuge in the God of Peace: The Trust of the Peacemaker

V. Give Us Peace, God of Peace: The Cry of the Peacemaker

VI. God Will Protect You on Your Journey of Peace: The Hope of the Peacemaker

VII. Praise Be Peace: The Song of the Peacemaker

VIII. Love and Truth Will Embrace; Justice and Peace Will Kiss: The Vision of the Peacemaker

GOD'S NAME IS PEACE.

The one who calls upon God's name to justify terrorism, violence, and war does not follow God's path. War in the name of religion becomes a war against religion itself. With firm resolve, therefore, let us reiterate that violence and terrorism are opposed to an authentic religious spirit.

POPE FRANCIS, ASSISI, SEPT. 20, 2016

The more deeply we grow into the psalms and the more often we pray them as our own, the more simple and rich will our prayer become.

DIETRICH BONHOEFFER

The most valuable thing the psalms do for me is to express the same delight in God which made David dance.

C.S. LEWIS

What's so powerful about the psalms are, as well as they're being gospel and songs of praise, they are also the blues.

BONO

To recognize that the psalms call us to pray and sing at the intersections of the times—of our time and God's time, of the then, and the now, and the not yet—is to understand how those emotions are to be held within the rhythm of a life lived in God's presence.

N.T. WRIGHT

Strange how repetition, reading the psalms each day, instead of becoming stale and repetitious, becomes even fresher: verses stand out, a light glows on what was obscure and hidden. There is an increase in understanding.

DOROTHY DAY

I grew to love the psalms. Day after day, year after year, they purified, blessed, set one moving to a rhythm that was by no means worldly or stereotyped or willful but lively and tranquil and passionately edgy. To pray the psalms with even half a heart was to be comforted and discomfited, set in motion, set in stillness, set free, set on edge, led outside, led within….The psalms spoke up for soul, for survival; they pled for all, they bonded us when the world would break us like dry bones.

DANIEL BERRIGAN

INTRODUCTION

D riving north along California's Highway One from my
little hermitage beside the Pacific Ocean near the village of
Harmony to Big Sur and its mountaintop New Camaldoli
monastery, I feel a lightness of spirit amid the breathtaking scenery and
the fresh ocean air. The vastness of the blue ocean, the shocking mountain cliffs, the mysterious rocky coast and sandy beaches, and the array
of creatures—the sea gulls, otters, curlews, dolphins, elephant seals,
whales, Stellar Jays, egrets, blue herons, and even the ten-foot-long, pre-
historic-looking condors—they toss away all worries and open a new
liminal space. Suddenly you find yourself in the best of God's creation.
Then almost without knowing it, you start longing for and looking for
the Creator of such peace.

Big Sur has long been a refuge for seekers and mystics. Thomas
Merton traveled up this road shortly before flying off to Asia and his
death. Joan Baez lived along this coast for years, and still lives just north.
Writers, poets, artists, and spiritually minded people dwell hidden away
along the mountain, while some four million people drive this magical
coastal road each year.

I've been coming here for over thirty years to visit the Catholic monastery on the top of the mountain. It's a difficult journey, one I take with a mixture of excitement and trepidation as I approach the steep cliff road. After Rocky Ridge and Limekiln, you come to the new road built after part of the mountain collapsed into the ocean in 2017. Then just before Lucia, you turn right onto a one-lane dirt road and start the hair-raising, life-threatening, cliff-hanging two mile zig-zag up the mountainside, tacking back and forth, until you come to the church, bookstore, guest rooms, and hermitages.

The drive up the mountain terrifies me because it's only one lane with no guard rails. The "road"—if you can call it that—continues to deteriorate, slowly slipping down the mountain, despite the repairs made every few months. But once on top, the vista catches your breath. You look out over the vast ocean, the miles of trees and tall grasses, down the mountain cliffs, and take a bird's-eye view of God's creation.

As you enter the old cinderblock chapel, Rublev's gentle icon of the Trinity seated around a table greets you. The white-robed monks are just gathering for one of their daily prayer vigils. They stand, face one another, and begin. "O God, come to my assistance," one chants. "O Lord, make haste to help me," they all respond.

At every prayer time, whether lauds or vigils, Mass or vespers, they turn to the psalms. In this way, they keep alive a two-thousand-year-old Christian tradition of prayer and song centered on these holy, ancient Jewish texts.

~~~

Thomas Merton held a romantic dream of the Camaldolese life. In the 1950s, he begged to leave his Trappist monastery of Gethsemani and join the Camaldolese, where each monk lives in silence and solitude, with his own private hermitage and garden, each close to the church where together they gather for daily prayer and Mass. Merton never left Gethsemani, but the Camaldolese way pushed him deeper into solitude and, eventually, to his own hermitage in the woods where he cultivated silence, peace, and grace.

St. Romuald founded the great monastery of Camaldoli in Tuscany under the Benedictine Rule over a thousand years ago. Only one text from St. Romuald survives, his "Little Rule":

> Sit in your cell as in paradise....Watch your thoughts like a good fisherman watching for fish. The path you must follow is in the psalms—never leave it. If you have just come to the monastery, and in spite of your good will you cannot accomplish what you want, then take every opportunity you can to sing the psalms in your heart and to understand them with your mind. And if your mind wanders as you read, do not give up. Hurry back and apply your mind to the words once more. Realize above all that you are in God's presence, and stand there. Empty yourself completely and sit waiting, content with the grace of God, like the chick who tastes nothing and eats nothing but what his mother brings him.

"Realize above all that you are in God's presence," Romuald writes, "and stand there." Be "content with the grace of God." Use the psalms as your daily text. For a thousand years, monks from St. Romuald to Thomas Merton have sat in that grace, emptied themselves into peace, chanted the psalms, and waited upon God. They not only walk the path to peace; they live the life of peace.

~~~

They say Jesus prayed the psalms regularly. He may have even known them by heart. If so, that's where he learned fearless devotion, dedicated truth, and total dependence on God. If you learn the psalms by heart, you set your heart and mind on God and God alone. For you, there is only God. For the rest of your life, there is only God. With

God, comes love, mercy, generosity, kindness, faithfulness, security, and peace toward yourself, your neighbor, all humanity, and all creation. In the psalms you hear the divine call to serve and liberate the poor and oppressed and establish universal peace with justice for every human being and all creation.

Jesus was meticulously nonviolent, so he must have brought to the psalms his own wisdom of nonviolence. The gospels begin with the story of Jesus' encounter with God after he was baptized at the Jordan River, where he heard in a moment of prayer a gentle loving God call him "My beloved." In that moment, Jesus knew God as loving, compassionate, and nonviolent. After that, he set forth on the gospel journey to invite everyone to welcome God's reign of peace and nonviolence here on earth. He stood up publicly and denounced the ways of empire and injustice and was crucified by the powers-that-be for his divine nonviolence and civil disobedience, but in his resurrection spirit, his campaign of nonviolence lives on.

The best way, then, to read the psalms is through the eyes of the nonviolent, compassionate Jesus, from a Gandhian/Kingian perspective of nonviolence, through the lens of the key gospel teachings—the Beatitudes and the Sermon on the Mount. If we read the psalms from Jesus' vision of nonviolence, we will find new strength to turn away from hate and anger toward greater trust and devotion to God and new-found wisdom, gratitude, and wonder.

Reading the psalms as Jesus read them can help us become more faithful, more devout, more fearless, more secure, more loving, more trusting, and more nonviolent. We learn not to place our trust in weapons or violence, not to act arrogantly or unjustly, not to doubt or test God. Instead, like Jesus, we will learn anew to place our security more and more in our gentle, loving God and discover the God of peace as our rock, our strength, our hope, our fortress, our security, and our protection. As we follow the nonviolent Jesus who prayed through the psalms, we learn to stand in faith, hope, and love, unarmed, vulnerable, nonviolent, our eyes focused on God, our hearts transformed like the Sacred Heart of Jesus, and our souls open to creation and the glories of heaven.

If we read the psalms from the perspective of gospel nonviolence, as Jesus advocates in the Sermon on the Mount, then these prayers take on new life. They make more sense. They lead us out of our inner violence into the spirit of peace, out of the culture of violence into a new culture of nonviolence, out of the world of death into the fullness of life in God.

They become just what we need.

~~~

The psalms are one hundred and fifty ancient prayers, about half of them attributed to David, evoking every emotion, from devotion and praise to anger and hatred, from vengeance and violence, despair and dread, to peace and glory. Many are liturgical prayers intended for the leader of a Jewish faith community. Some are hymns of praise. Others offer thanksgiving. Many are individual or communal lamentations. Fundamentally, they are an ancient cry to God, and as such, they are as relevant today as ever.

With sisters and brothers of old, we, too, cry out to God for help and protection, for security and comfort, for justice and peace. We, too, wrestle with both our faith and our emotions in our daily struggles, fears, crises, and breakdowns, as we endure the world's permanent wars, racism and sexism, corporate greed, killings, systemic injustice, and environmental destruction. Like the nonviolent Jesus, we strive to be compassionate and nonviolent, to do our part to bring justice and peace, and to make the world decent and sane.

For two thousand years, Christians have read the psalms as a basic form of prayer. Priests, nuns, and members of religious orders in particular still read them every single day. They unite the prayer of the global church in a cry for help, a hymn of praise, and a pledge of trust. But for some seventeen hundred years, we Christians have neglected the nonviolence of Jesus, and so we have often been misled by the violence in the psalms and other texts to believe in a false god of violence.

Jesus brought his extraordinary vision of universal love, boundless compassion, and total nonviolence to every person, every moment, every situation in life—and so, I presume, even to the Scriptures. He announced that he was the fullness of the law and the prophets, that his understanding of God reached beyond our limited understanding to behold a nonviolent God, a God who does not hate, does not kill, does not want us to suffer injustice. The God of the nonviolent Jesus is a God of unconditional, nonviolent, all-encompassing, all-embracing, all-inclusive universal love and peace. As he prayed through the psalms, Jesus must have found encouragement, strength, and hope to go forward and be faithful to who he was—the beloved of God, sent to proclaim God's reign of peace.

His was a daily life-and-death struggle to resist the culture of violence and propose an entirely new world of nonviolence, which he called "the reign of God at hand." The psalms were his prayer book, so they must have helped him fulfill his mission, trust in God no matter what, endure risk and misunderstanding with patience and faith, and lay down his life for God and humanity in a spirit of loving nonviolence. If that is the Christian calling—to follow Jesus on his public campaign of nonviolence—then the psalms can help us too as we try to carry our own public campaigns of creative nonviolence for justice and creation.

~~~

Alas, some verses in the psalms clearly espouse violence and uphold a violent god as if violence were a sacred, religious duty. "Blessed are those who seize your children and smash them against a rock," we read

(137:9). "God will crush the skulls of the enemy" (68:22). "Slay my enemies, God" (59:12). "March with our armies, God" (108:12).

I suggest the time has come to drop these verses from our prayer, to reject any biblical call to violence, and to adhere only to those texts that help us become people of loving nonviolence, like Jesus. Of course, I'm not the only one who thinks this.

Shortly before he died, legendary Benedictine monk and interfaith leader Bede Griffiths wrote a book about the psalms where he announced that after a lifetime of praying the psalms every single day, he now realized that some verses should no longer be recited by Christians. We Christians are summoned to be as nonviolent as Christ, he argued, and so we need to avoid anything and everything that promotes violence, including scriptural texts calling for violence and war. Bede Griffiths was one of the first major religious figures in modern history to make this bold suggestion, and I think we should take his advice to heart:

> It has become more and more difficult to accept many of the Psalms as Christian prayers. Taken in their literal sense many of the Psalms express feelings of anger, hatred and revenge against one's enemies which are entirely opposed to the teaching of the gospel on love of one's enemies. ... It has become urgent, therefore, to revise the Psalter, so that all branding of others as "enemies," "wicked" and "sinners" deserving no mercy or pity, should be removed. When one considers the incalculable harm which has resulted from this habit of mind in the Church, as seen in the Inquisition, the Crusades, the wars of religion and the persecution of "heretics," it is clear that a revision of this kind is urgently needed. (Bede Griffiths, *Psalms for Christian Prayer*, Harper Collins, 1995, vii–x)

Bede Griffiths makes the case that Christians who love the psalms need to remember the nonviolence of Jesus and adhere to the boundaries of nonviolence, even in the way we pray and understand God.

~~~

At the monastery in Big Sur, when the monks chant the psalms, one of them sings the first line, and then the others join in. "Out of the depths I cry to you, O Lord," they sing. My friend the prior tells me that when they start singing the psalms, he enters a dream. It's as if, for him, the psalms are a door into the Cloud of Unknowing, into the Mystery of the Divine, into the Holy Spirit. He lets the psalms wash over him, through him, and under him so that he finds himself "content in grace," in the peace of God, waiting, hoping, looking, loving, and being. For the monks, these prayers are the doorway to the fullness of life and grace.

In this book, I offer reflections on various key psalms from the perspective of gospel nonviolence so that you too might find new strength from these ancient prayers to follow the nonviolent Jesus more and more on the path of peace and to be content in grace. May these pages encourage you on your journey and lead you to even greater blessings of peace.

J.D.
Big Sur, California

I

Seek Peace and Pursue It

THE CALLING OF
THE PEACEMAKER

*Trust in the God of peace and do good
that you may dwell in the land and live secure.
Take delight in the God of peace
who will give you your heart's desire....
Those at peace with God have a future.*
PSALM 37

1 Seek Peace and Pursue It

PSALM 34

Come, children, listen to me. I will teach you awe
of the God of peace.
Who among you loves life, takes delight in prosperous days?
Keep your tongue from evil, your lips from speaking lies.
Turn from evil and do good. Seek peace and pursue it.

In the early 1980s, I started a correspondence with someone on Georgia's death row. When he was nineteen, he robbed a liquor store late one night because he had no money. He panicked and shot and killed the elderly store owner. He immediately fell to the ground, wept over what he had done, repented of his action, and asked the man's family to forgive him. They did, but he went on to spend many years on death row. On at least three occasions, he came within a few hours of execution.

We became friends, and so, after a few years, I flew to Georgia and spent a day visiting him on death row. Then, in July 1990, a week before he was scheduled to be executed, he sent a message asking me to accompany him and to be there with him as he was killed. I agreed and flew to Georgia. With two other friends, we organized a series of public prayer vigils and, the day before his scheduled execution, attended the public hearing of the Georgia Board of Pardon and Paroles. There, the victim's family pleaded for my friend's life, and so, for the first time in Georgia's history, the Board granted clemency. A month later, my friend was released from prison. Today, he is happily married with children and serves as a minister in a church in Georgia. We remain friends.

Years before, though, our correspondence had a rocky start. I was a brash young whippersnapper, quite full of myself, arrogant and pompous. I wanted to support someone on death row and was given his address.

I wrote him condescendingly, saying in effect, "I'm a very busy person, have many difficulties with graduate school and peace activism, but I wanted to offer you my support." He wrote back immediately to thank me for my letter and said right at the start: "I'm fine. My life is under the complete control of our Lord Jesus. You, on the other hand, sound like you're a mess. Maybe I should be the one to support you. How can I help you?"

I was stunned. I wrote right back, denying my need for help, but he answered saying that it was obvious who the person in need was. And so, for nearly a decade, he wrote almost weekly advising me, encouraging me, and praying for me. He urged me to place my life in God's hands and not to worry or be anxious or fearful. He said that he learned this profound level of trust in God by praying through Psalm 34 every day on death row.

And so, we begin with Psalm 34, since it was taught to me at an early age by my friend and teacher and became one of the first psalms to take root in me. It reads like a hymn of praise, a guide to daily living, an invitation to wisdom, as well as a testimony to God's liberation of the poor and oppressed. In these turbulent times, it can help us surrender more and more to the God of peace and find deeper inner peace, come what may.

~~~

The first part of Psalm 34 is an invitation to join in permanent praise for the God of peace:

> *I will bless the God of peace at all times;*
> *God's praise shall be always in my mouth.*
> *My soul will glory in the God of peace that the poor*
> *   may hear and be glad.*
> *Praise the God of peace with me.*

Psalm 34 sets a goal for our lives: spend every day of your life from now on blessing the God of peace. We bless, praise, glorify, honor, and adore the God of peace and God's gift of peace. That means we do not honor war, hatred, revenge, resentments, domination, or empire. We honor and praise and worship the God whose name is Peace.

In order to praise the God of peace, we have to turn away from the culture of war and greed. The God of peace gets our full attention. As we seek God's peace, we start to side more and more with the poor, the marginalized, and the enemy, and we share God's peace with them by working for justice and disarmament. We learn that God is on the side of the poor and oppressed, the peacemakers and justice-seekers, not the rich and the oppressor, the warmakers or injustice-makers. So we announce that God is on the side of the poor and oppressed, on the side of peace and justice. In other words, as we surrender our hearts and lives to the God of peace, we open ourselves to the social, economic, and political implications of active peacemaking in the world. We try to embrace the whole human race with God, and that means we side with everyone in universal love, beginning with the poor, the marginalized, and the enemies of our nation.

～～～

The second part of the psalms testifies that God helps us in our time of need and urges us to call upon and rely on the God of peace:

> I sought the God of peace who answered me,
> delivered me from all my fears... .
> In my misfortune I called;
> the God of peace heard and saved me from all distress... .
> Look to the God of peace that you may be radiant with joy.
> Learn to savor how good the God of peace is.
> Blessed are those who take refuge in God.
> Those who seek the God of peace lack no good thing.

If we trust in the God of peace and turn to the God of peace in good times and in bad, God will help us, deliver us, and save us—that's the message, the testimony, the promise. We're told that God delivers all those who turn toward God, especially the poor, the oppressed, the brokenhearted and the crushed, which means all of us. That means, of course, that we too are called to be on the side of the poor, the oppressed, the brokenhearted, and the crushed. We are invited to recognize our own poverty, brokenness, and need for God. If we call upon God, God will help us.

If we call upon God regularly, we will discover God's abiding care as a fundamental permanent gift, and we will rejoice and savor how beautiful the God of peace is, how kind and gentle, how loving to us all.

I like this word "savor." Imagine savoring a delicious meal, a glass of fine wine, or a stunning sunset. Here, we're invited to "savor" the goodness of the God of peace. As we take time to ponder and wonder over God's goodness, we might notice the time and attention we give to savoring other things, such as bad news, disappointments, grudges, or the nation. Instead of savoring what is not good, we can discipline ourselves to savor what is good, most especially, the great goodness of the God of peace.

The more we ponder the goodness of God, the more we come to know God as goodness itself. God does not have a trace of evil, or mean-spiritedness, or war, or hatred. The act of savoring God's goodness can heal our brokenness and help us reclaim our own inherent goodness, recenter ourselves in goodness, and live in goodness. We become do-gooders and share the goodness of God far and wide.

~~~

The third part lists the essential instructions on how to live well, how to be centered on the God of peace, how to love life and how to take delight in good days. These instructions are worth studying and following:

> Come, children, listen to me; I will teach you awe
> > for the God of peace.
> Who among you loves life, takes delight in prosperous days?
> Keep your tongue from evil, your lips from speaking lies.
> Depart from evil and do good.
> Seek peace, and pursue it.

It is interesting to note that the first precept is *Do not speak evil or lies*. In other words, only speak goodness, kindness, truth, and love. Choose your words carefully, the psalmist instructs, so that you do not spread the culture's untruth, reinforce evil, and hurt others. Use words wisely, nonviolently, mindfully, because words have the power to heal or destroy.

As we become more mindful about the words we use and the things we say, we notice what we talk about, and we choose to speak about the deeper things—the call to love, peace, and nonviolence, the need for justice and disarmament, the fate of Mother Earth and the creatures, the sufferings of the poor and oppressed, the glories of God. We talk about these good things and denounce the culture of violence and war; and in doing so, we lend our voices to the global grassroots movement of nonviolence working for a new culture of peace and nonviolence. As we speak the language of truth, peace, and goodness, we help spread nonviolence and encourage people everywhere to pursue a new world of truth, nonviolence, and peace.

Turn from evil and do good. This teaching is one of the fundamental tasks of the spiritual life—to turn from evil and do good. Every day, we're called to turn away from evil, to stop doing evil, to avoid evil, and from now on to do good. I would add St. Paul's addendum that we try to overcome evil with goodness. In other words, we do good, turn from evil, and seek to transform evil into goodness through the power of nonviolent love, which is the heart and methodology of goodness.

As we hear this call to turn from evil and do good, we have to take stock of our hearts and lives and fearlessly examine our behavior to see how we do evil or good, and then take action so that we stop doing evil and do only the good. That may mean quitting an unjust job; leaving the military; renouncing the social sins of racism, sexism, and greed; getting rid of our guns; turning off the television; and cultivating peace and goodness as the priority of our lives. We want to stop any behavior that is violent toward ourselves, such as smoking or taking drugs; stop any violent behavior toward others, such as yelling at people or putting people down; and stop any participation in the culture of violence, such as owning guns or supporting war, so that our lives, which are good, publicly do the good. To do the good at the highest level, we have to join the various grassroots movements for justice, disarmament, and creation, to "organize goodness," as Dr. King called it.

Seek peace and pursue it. Seeking peace and pursuing peace is another way to speak of the spiritual life, the lifelong pilgrimage to the God of peace. This is the meaning, purpose, and wisdom of life: to live at peace with oneself, to cultivate interior peace, to make peace with the God of peace; to live in peace with all peoples and all creatures; and even to seek peace with all nations, the whole human race, and Mother Earth.

As peace-seekers, we take time every day for peace, for the God of peace. That means we practice daily meditation as an ordinary part of our lives. In meditation, we sit quietly with ourselves, until we start to settle down into peace, into the God of peace, so that the God of peace can breathe through us, dwell within us, and use us. Meditation is the doorway to peace. For all seekers, it becomes an ordinary, essential ingredient in our lives. In our meditation, we learn to still the voices in our head, to rest in peace, to listen to the God of peace, and to breathe in peace.

To seek peace and pursue it means of course that we do not seek war or pursue war. That means we non-cooperate with every type of violence, every aspect of the culture of war. We do not cultivate war with ourselves, our spouses, our children, our relatives, our neighbors; with those who are different from us; with those who live in different lands, nations, or cultures. We do not make war upon the creatures or Mother Earth. We do not own, build, or support any weapons of violence or war. And we do not remain silent in the face of violence or war.

Our pursuit of peace includes a public stand for peace, which means we speak out publicly for disarmament, justice, the poor of the world, and Mother Earth. We do our part to support the global grassroots movements of peace, justice, and nonviolence, and so we do our little part to help end war, such as the ongoing US wars in Afghanistan, Iraq, Yemen, Syria, and Palestine. We work to end the big business of war, to abolish nuclear weapons, to eradicate hunger, poverty, and racism, which sow the seeds of war, and to stop environmental destruction.

The combination of these teachings leads us further along the path of nonviolence. Speak the truth, turn from evil, do good, and seek peace. Eventually, we learn to "speak, turn, do, and seek" all the time, so that every thought, word, and deed becomes an expression of peace, of the God of peace, and we become true peacemakers.

~~~

After urging us to turn from evil, seek peace, and pursue it, the fourth part of the psalm describes the nature of God, giving us a new fundamental understanding of God as the God of peace and justice and the spiritual basis for our work for peace and justice:

> *The God of peace has eyes for the just and ears for their cry.*
> *God's face is against evildoers to wipe out their memory*
> *from the earth. When the just cry out,*

the God of peace hears and rescues them from all their troubles.
The God of peace is close to the brokenhearted,
saves those whose spirit is crushed.
Many are the afflictions of the just, but the God of peace delivers
from them all.

In the end, Psalm 34 summons us to serve the God of peace, bless the God of peace, trust the God of peace, and spend our lives turning away from evil and doing peace and goodness. It serves as a basic reminder for our spiritual lives, for how to be human, for how to go forward in peace and goodness in a world of war and evil.

"Blessed are those who take refuge in the God of peace," Psalm 34 advises. With that blessing, we set our hearts and souls in the God of peace and reframe our lives to live always in the presence and practice of the God of peace.

2   Teach Us to Count Our Days Aright
PSALM 90

Teach us to count our days,
that we may gain wisdom of heart.
Fill us at daybreak with your mercy,
that all our days we may sing for joy.

I became aware of Psalm 90 in my early twenties. I noticed it's urgent call, and it dogged me. I decided to hear its lesson: Life is short. Don't waste your one precious life. Wake up, live wisely, spend your days in the service of God and humanity. Otherwise, before you know it, it will be over and you will find that you never lived.

Thinking about death when I was young, I noticed that no one was ever able to avoid it. As far as I could tell, no one who ever lived did not at some point die. Despite this, few people ever talked about death, even though it surrounded us, what with the Vietnam War, nuclear weapons, and cancer. I was scared of death, but over the years I became familiar with it. I accompanied several people to their deaths, traveled extensively in war zones, knew people who were publicly assassinated or executed on death row, and even faced down death squads in El Salvador and elsewhere. I wanted to resist the forces of death but quickly learned that if you were going to spend your life resisting death, you better learn how to live life to the full.

It is astonishing how we go through life never talking about death, pretending we will not die, acting as if we will live forever. We think we are immortal. I don't think ignoring the reality of death helps. The culture of death wants to keep us ignorant about death so it can plow ahead with its global campaign of bringing good people to death through war, poverty, and violence. It hypnotizes us to go through life as sleepwalkers, unaware that our days are numbered, quietly supporting militarism, nationalism, consumerism, and materialism, and ignoring the early and unjust deaths of so many sisters and brothers.

The spiritual life faces the reality of life and death head on. It is life to the full, life lived in pursuit of the God of life, life lived so that all others might share the fullness of life, and therefore a life that non-cooperates with the forces of death. A fully human life understands its limits and chooses wisely, therefore, not to waste a single moment. It recognizes the reality of death and so lives life to the full by working to stop the forces of death killing so many others.

That's the call of Psalm 90. As I read the psalm from the perspective of the nonviolent Jesus, I ignore talk about God's wrath and focus on its reminder about the shortness of life and the challenge to live wisely and well:

Our years come to an end like a sigh.
Seventy is the sum of our years,
or eighty, if we are strong;
most of them are toil and sorrow;
they pass quickly, and we are gone.

At best, you might make it to eighty, the psalmist reminds us. You will work hard, know sorrow, then get sick and die. There is no way around this inevitable mysterious reality. At some point, your body will fail you and stop working. That is, if you don't die earlier from some disease or accident or violence.

Most of us numb ourselves to this truth. We drink, take drugs, and give in to addiction to anesthetize ourselves. Then one day we realize that time has flown by and illness and death are upon us. We ask why, we rage in anger, we sink into depression, and we complain in misery. The denial of death does not help us avoid it or undergo it well with grace, wisdom, and peace. It just keeps us anesthetized and so muddies the meaning, wonder, and potential of our one precious gift.

"Wake up!" Psalm 90 says. "Your one life is a precious gift! Live it wisely! Live every day to the full! Live for the God of peace, at peace with the God of peace, at peace with all humanity and creation!" To that end, it offers one of the key teachings of the Bible:

Teach us to count our days aright,
that we may gain wisdom of heart.
Fill us at daybreak with your mercy,
that all our days we may sing for joy.
May the favor of the God of peace be upon us.

Instead of ignoring life and death, Psalm 90 encourages us to pray for the grace to count our days aright, that is, to live wisely and attentively every day of our lives, to be aware of the precious gift of life and to make the most of our lives as a gift to God and humanity, to treasure every moment with every human being in this Garden of Eden.

The psalmist wants us to receive the gift of "wisdom of heart," a beautiful phrase that invites us to live fully with wise hearts, so that we might practice the wisdom of universal love, compassion, and nonviolence. With "wisdom of heart," we practice daily mindfulness in the present moment. We try to live consciously in full awareness of the precious gift of life and, therefore, to serve others and make life beautiful and peaceful for others. If we cultivate wisdom of heart, we open our hearts in universal love, compassion, and nonviolence toward every human being, all creatures, and Mother Earth and surrender our lives to the God of peace. This pleases God and leads to new blessings for ourselves and others. We will be blessed with mercy and joy and find favor with God and creation. What a blessing!

3 Teach Me Your Way, God of Peace
PSALMS 86, 25

Teach me your way, God of peace, that I may walk in your truth,
single-hearted and revering your name.
Give strength to your servant.

The primary task for us as Christians is to follow the nonviolent Jesus on the path of peace. He is our way, our truth, our life, and our peace. But to follow the nonviolent Jesus along the Way, as the Way, we have to ask for the grace to learn his way, to know his way, and to walk his way. And then, as we embark on his way, we ask for the grace to remain on the way, to stay faithful to the way, to maintain the strength to walk the way for the rest of our lives.

That's the prayer of Psalm 86, and Psalm 25 as well. It's a theme that runs throughout the Psalms. "You alone, God of peace, are God. Teach me your way, God of peace, that I may walk in your truth." One of the basic prayers of the Psalms is a request of the God of peace to teach us God's way, that we might learn God's teachings, put them into practice, and walk God's way for the rest of our lives.

But why does the psalmist ask God to teach God's way? Perhaps having to ask reveals how much we fundamentally do not want to learn God's way. What if we really learned God's way and put it into practice in our lives? What would that mean for our lives? How much would we have to change? How far will we go to resist changing ourselves?

This is why we pray for the grace to be taught, to become "teachable." Few of us are "teachable." This characteristic requires a certain openness, generosity, and curiosity about life and wisdom. It demands a willingness to hear, learn, and change. That fundamental attitude of "teachableness" is the hallmark of nonviolence. We do not resort to the same old useless ways of violence. We are creative, open, nonviolent. We want to learn and, most important, to learn from God.

If we want to be taught God's way, as followers of the nonviolent Jesus, then a good response to this psalm is to sit down and reread the Sermon on the Mount (Matthew 5—7), where the basic teachings of Jesus are gathered. If Jesus is the fullest revelation of God, then these basic teachings are God's way for us. They are clear and decidedly countercultural. Perhaps that is why we ignore them so consistently and rarely ask God or Jesus to teach us.

But you and I want to rise above ourselves and the culture. We want to be taught by God. We choose to hear the teachings, take them to heart, and put them into practice, starting with ourselves. That's why this psalm is so helpful. It sets us at the beginning every time we read it, asking for the grace to be taught the wisdom of God, that we might walk in God's way.

Notice the word "single-hearted." We ask to be single-hearted, to have hearts focused solely on the God of peace, set in God's universal peace on the path to God. With this steadfast devotion, we can say, "I will praise you with all my heart." In that way, we become wholehearted servants, set on the God of peace.

Notice, too, how we remind God of God's true qualities—mercy, compassion, and graciousness. "Your mercy to me is great," we pray. "You are a compassionate and gracious God, slow to anger, abounding in mercy and truth. This is who you are. You are the God of mercy, the God of compassion, the God of truth, the God of universal love, the God of nonviolence. And so, be gracious to me, give me the strength to walk your way of mercy, compassion, truth, love, and nonviolence for the rest of my life." That is the prayer of the peacemaker. The peacemaker knows that God is first and foremost a peacemaker.

When we ask to learn the teachings of God and walk in God's way, we are asking to be sent by the God of peace into the culture of war as God's pilgrims of peace who walk the path of peace, come what may, spreading God's teachings of peace, mercy, and nonviolence. This is the fulfilling mission of the peacemaker, the one sent by the risen nonviolent Jesus to carry on his campaign of nonviolence.

~~~

Psalm 25 offers the same prayer. Both psalms remind us of the importance of asking God to teach us God's way, to lead us on God's way, and to give us the strength to remain on God's way.

> *Make known to me your ways, God of peace.*
> *Teach me your paths.*
> *Lead me by your fidelity and teach me,*
> *for you are God my savior,*
> *for you I wait all day long.*

Remember your compassion and your mercy,
for they are ages old.
Remember me according to your mercy,
because of your goodness.
Good and upright is the God of peace;
therefore, God shows sinners the way.
God guides the humble in righteousness,
and leads the humble God's way.
All the paths of the God of peace are mercy and truth
toward those who honor God's covenant and decrees.

Psalm 25 adds that God guides the humble and teaches the humble God's way. If we are proud, arrogant, narcissistic, and self-centered, we will not learn God's way. We will never ask to be taught God's way. We will follow our own way and unconsciously go our own way. Learning and following God's way requires humility. It means admitting that we do not know the way of God, that we need to be taught, that God's way is better than our misguided way, and that we need God's guidance to live along God's way. That's a helpful insight. Prayer and teachableness require that we humble ourselves before God and confess our ignorance. That is not a put-down or an act of low self-esteem. On the contrary, wisdom begins with humility.

In humility, we find doors that open into God. In humility, we remember that we have a brief time on earth to serve others and God. In humility, we discover the wisdom of peace, love, and nonviolence. In humility, we encounter the loving God who takes notice of us, cares for us, and guides us through our lives. In humility, we welcome God's gift of peace and take it to heart.

4 Blessed Is the One Who Does Justice
PSALM 112

Blessed is the one who greatly delights in the commands
    of the God of peace.
Light rises through the darkness for the upright;
the God of peace is gracious, compassionate, and righteous.
It is good for the person gracious in lending,
who conducts affairs with justice.
That one shall never be shaken and shall be remembered forever.
Never fearing an ill report; the righteous person's heart
    is steadfast,
tranquil, without fear, trusting the God of peace.
Lavishly giving to the poor, the righteous one shall endure forever.

Psalm 112 invites us to be people who live just and upright lives, who make justice a hallmark, who seek justice for others. Justice people serve the poor, advocate for justice, speak out against injustice, and remain fearless and steadfast. According to the psalm, they live in the light and delight in God's way of justice and peace. They can't help it. That's who they are.

This teaching—to live on the side of justice—is important first of all because the world is so unjust. Billions of people suffer in poverty, hunger, and warfare, through no fault of their own, while a handful of us live comfortable lives. To be a just person is to take a public stand for justice, to side with the world's poor, to do our best to advocate for justice, to speak out publicly against systemic injustice in every form, and to make our lives a light rising in the darkness. This is not easy. We can't delude ourselves into thinking that we are just if we are not involved with the poor and the struggle for justice. It also does no good to think that working for justice is impossible because no one can really make a difference; then we might as well give up before we even start. The whole point of the spirituality of justice is that we try our best—and keep trying come what may.

Doing justice is the daily struggle to get out of our comfort zones and stand with those in pain and sorrow in the grassroots movements for human rights, dignity, fairness, and peace. It means taking sides on behalf of the world's poor and oppressed, however unpopular that side is. It means living not for ourselves, but first and foremost for others, especially those in need, for our suffering sisters and brothers around the world. This is what it means to be human.

Think of those you know who are just, who take time to serve the poor and needy, who actively participate in the grassroots movements for justice and peace. Notice how doing justice and peace has become an ordinary way of life for them, even if they seem to make little headway. That ordinary life of justice is favored by God, according to Psalm 112. It is the heart of the spiritual life, of religious practice, and of a meaningful life. Sustaining such a life requires getting together with other like-minded justice-seekers and joining a local justice and peace group. As we work with others, we find not only that we can sustain and deepen our commitment to justice but that we can actually make a difference in the lives of those who need help.

If we choose to live on the side of justice, then we are freed from fear. That is one of the teachings here. We need not fear anything or anyone. We know that God blesses justice and that God will use us for God's work of justice. We need only trust in God, dwell in the light, and be at peace. Our hearts can be steadfast and tranquil, because we are like God, on the side of the poor and oppressed people. Such a one is never shaken, the psalm declares. As we strive to be solid and steadfast, we learn over time to let go of our fears, to live in fearlessness, and to cultivate graciousness and peace. As we struggle for justice, the psalm teaches, we cultivate interior tranquility and personal equanimity. In this way, our lives become a gift for others, and we give greater glory to God.

Easy for you to say, you're thinking. No, I find this devilishly hard.

On the one hand, we're called to do justice, serve the poor, and take a stand against injustice; on the other hand, we're called to be tranquil and gracious. Most of us are good at one of these, but balancing both is a high-wire tightrope walk that requires steady vigilance. The saints managed to do both. They served the poor and spoke for justice while at the same time remaining kind, gracious, and peaceful. It's a difficult challenge, but they show us that it's possible, and so we do our best and discover new blessings.

II

The God of Peace Ends All Wars

THE FAITH OF THE PEACEMAKER

*Too long have I lived
among those who hate peace.
I am for peace, but when I speak,
they are for war.*
PSALM 120

*Come and behold the works of the God of peace
who stops wars to the ends of the earth,
breaks the war bow, shatters the war spear,
and burns the shields with fire,
who says, "Be still and know that I am the God of peace."*
PSALM 46

5 "A King Is Not Saved by a Mighty Army; Neither Are We" ☀ PSALM 33

A king is not saved by a great army, nor a warrior delivered
by great strength.
Useless is the war horse for safety; its great strength, no sure escape.
But the eyes of the God of peace are upon the reverent,
upon those who count on God's gracious help.

Psalm 33 is a hymn of praise to the God of peace and a warning to those who place their hope and trust in the false gods of war. You can't serve both the God of peace and the weapons of war, it announces. It's one or the other. Show reverence to the God of peace and live in peace, gratitude, and joy, or show reverence to the weapons of war and their false security and die. That's the message I get from the text. It's more radical—and helpful—than any spiritual writing you'll find today.

No, you say, this is just pious Bible talk. A king, an emperor, a president *are* saved by a mighty army, by bombs, by drones, by Trident submarines, by nuclear weapons. That is the logic of every nation, every military, every war. The God of peace cannot save us. Only our weapons and warriors can save us. This is what we have been taught, what we hear preached, why we wave the flag, why we pay taxes for the Pentagon, why we risk radioactive waste, why we threaten to destroy the planet, why we spend nearly all our money on warfare instead of on schools, healthcare, affordable housing, food for the hungry, and environmental cleanup. This is what most of us believe. Might makes right. Violence saves us. War is the will of God. Our weapons are our only protection.

Not too long ago, a US archbishop said these exact words to me: "God cannot save us. Only nuclear weapons can protect us. They are our only hope." I consider such talk pure blasphemy. Such a statement reveals a lack of faith in the God of peace.

Even if you believe in the power of violent weapons to "save" you, what does that mean? Napoleon still died. Hitler, Stalin, Mussolini all still died, despite all their military might. Harry Truman was "jubilant" when he announced that he had vaporized two hundred thousand people in Hiroshima and Nagasaki, but he still died twenty-five years later. War and weapons do not save you from death or the moment when you meet your Maker. They only assure you that you violate every teaching of the nonviolent Jesus about the God of peace. In that case, even if you are unsure about the power of war and weapons, a look at today's news proves that they have not made the world safer; so we might as well try another option—structured, funded, international nonviolent conflict resolution as a way to solve all international crises nonviolently. The good news is that statistical research now proves that where nonviolent conflict resolution was tried, there was a much higher likelihood of a more just, more peaceful outcome and longer-lasting democracy.

In other words: war doesn't work. It's time we tried the ancient teachings of peace as the way to peace.

~~~

Trust in the weapons of war and the US military has now reached unimaginable heights. Annual world military spending in 2015 hit $1.6 trillion dollars. The United States spends 37 percent of that, more than the seven next largest military economies combined—China, Saudi Arabia, Russia, Britain, India, France, and Japan.

In recent years, US taxpayers spent $121 billion for ongoing warfare in Afghanistan and Iraq. One report I read said that specific amount could have provided 1.8 million US elementary school teachers for one year, or 15.5 million people with low income health care for one year, or 15.4 million one-year student scholarships to attend university. When we trust in the weapons of war, we waste our money on useless weapons of death and not on schools, health care, low-income housing, food for the hungry, clean water, and environmental sustainability. And we still find ourselves no safer from a coordinated terrorist attack, even despite our nuclear arsenal.

From 2001 to 2011, we spent about $1.4 trillion for war in Iraq and Afghanistan. Another report I read said that same amount of money would have provided universal health care for all Americans for those same ten years. What have these wars brought us? Over 6,400 US service members killed in Iraq and Afghanistan; over 300,000 service members with traumatic brain injuries and PTSD. Civilian deaths estimated in the hundreds of thousands. And still, the United States ranks twenty-fifth in the world in infant mortality; thirty-seventh in the world in overall health care; seventeenth in the world in terms of life expectancy; we have the highest rate of childhood poverty in the industrialized world. And we are certainly not any safer or more secure because of this military spending and killing.

A few years ago, under the presidency of Barack Obama, Republicans and Democrats in Congress united to approve a $1 trillion upgrade in the US nuclear weapons arsenal over the next few decades. The United States says our ultimate security is nuclear weapons. If we believed in God, and placed our security in God and God's way of peacemaking, we would not spend one more dime on nuclear weapons. Instead we would dismantle our arsenal and invest in food, housing, education, health care, jobs, and dignity for everyone at home and abroad and fund a new culture of peace and nonviolence. You can't fund such a culture when all your money goes into building and maintaining weapons of mass destruction. In fact, we are headed toward bankruptcy.

~~~

Psalm 33 presents a stark challenge. Reliance on war, funding for war, and waging war are futile. If you place your hope in war, then know that you are not placing your hope in the God of peace. If you trust in weapons and warfare for your security, then know that you are not trusting in the God of peace, and you are doomed to failure and death.

This truth is presented as if it is a law of nature, like a law of gravity. Jesus picks up on the message when he says: If you live by the sword, the weapon, the bomb, you will die by the sword, the weapon, the bomb. Therefore, do not live by the sword, the weapon, or the bomb. Live in my peace, he says, and you will live. This is the first requirement of the spiritual life, the politics of the spiritual life: renounce warfare and take up the way of peace. Welcome Jesus' resurrection gift of peace and you will enter the fullness of life.

You can't have it both ways; it's either war or peace.

Can we build our lives on this sacred text? Could we fashion a Judeo-Christian culture of peace after these words? What have we got to lose? The world remains stuck in permanent warfare, poverty, and racism, but now with our nuclear arsenal and catastrophic climate change upon us, we are in greater danger than ever. Our weapons have failed us. I hope we can take the risk of speaking out and rejecting the culture of violence and war and pursue a new culture of nonviolence and peace. That's what Psalm 33 suggests.

The nonviolent Jesus must have studied and prayed through this text because it provides the basic foundation for his Sermon on the Mount. If we likewise pray over and ponder these words, then perhaps we would fulfill the Sermon on the Mount and help end war; dismantle our weapons; create social, racial, and economic justice; and offer universal peace to everyone.

～

Let all who dwell in the world show reverence....
The God of peace foils the plan of the nations....

From heaven, the God of peace looks down
and observes the whole human race,
surveying from the royal throne all who live on earth.
The One who fashioned the hearts of them all knows
  all their works.

Psalm 33 insists that the God of peace sees the violence we commit and the wars we wage. This living God of peace and nonviolence knows what we are doing to destroy one another and creation. The summons is to get on the side of the God of peace and welcome God's reign of peace with gratitude, joy, and praise. But the specific word it uses is *reverence*.

Twice, Psalm 33 invites us to become people of *reverence*. That was one of Albert Schweitzer's favorite words. As people of reverence, we maintain an attitude of deep respect, love, and awe for the God of peace. We venerate the God of peace. We manifest our respect, love, and awe for the God of peace by the way we live. That means we are focused on the God of peace. We bow toward the God of peace. We live in, and through, and for the God of peace. We defer to the God of peace. We seek the God of peace. We breathe in the God of peace and speak and heed the words of the God of peace.

We place all our trust in the God of peace. We know that God will help us as we need, and so we hope in God. "The eyes of the God of peace are upon the reverent," we are told, "upon those who hope for God's gracious help."

In this spirit of reverence, we take time each day for silent adoration of the God of peace. Then we go through our day with one eye—our third eye, the Buddhists would say—on the God of peace. As we keep our eye on the God of peace, the God of peace keeps both eyes on us. What a blessing!

People of reverence are people of mindfulness, peaceableness, non-violence, love, and compassion. Living in reverence leads to equanimity because we are rooted in our attitude of respect, love, and awe for the God of peace. This is a good way to live. We need not support the culture of war or be tossed about by the media's glorification of violence, war, or corrupt corporate politics or our own day-to-day worries and anxieties. We remain centered, mindful, conscious, and alert, and so we maintain our basic reverence for peace.

I think many of us want to be people of reverence, but we also want at the same time to maintain our American culture, its weapons, its wars, its armies, and the Pentagon. Psalm 33 insists that we cannot have it both ways. Reject the culture of war, it commands. Learn new ways to resolve conflict nonviolently, and return to the God of peace. Then you will be able to reclaim your soul and live in the deep foundation of peace with the God of peace. This psalm insists we can do this, that we need not have it both ways, that we can truly be people of peace, who love and serve the God of peace, first and foremost, from now on. I think that's worth striving for.

~~~

Our soul waits for the God of peace, who is our help and shield.
For in the God of peace our hearts rejoice.
In your holy name we trust.
May your kindness, God of peace, be upon us.
We have put our hope in you.

This is the pledge and the prayer of the political, antimilitary, antiwar Psalm 33. Instead of trusting in America, its military, its drones, and its nuclear weapons, we pledge to wait on the God of peace and trust in this peacemaking God to help us and protect us. As we do, we will be given a quiet, inner joy.

And so we pray: "God of peace, may your kindness be upon us!" That could be our new mantra. It invites us to imagine the kindness of

God—and then to feel it upon us, within us, and around us. Then we become kinder people, people of loving nonviolence who practice a politics of kindness rooted in nonviolence, disarmament, and justice for all.

Psalm 33 suggests that if we turn away from the culture of war, renounce our reliance on weapons, and practice a new reverence for the God of peace, one another, and all creation, then the kindness of the God of peace will rest on us. That is a promise worth pursuing.

6 "God Stops Wars to the Ends of the Earth" ☀ PSALM 46

Come and see the works of the God of peace who has done awesome
    deeds on earth,
who stops wars to the ends of the earth, breaks the war bow,
shatters the war spear, and burns the shields with fire,
who says: "Be still and know that I am the God of peace."

How refreshing to hear this verse, right in the center of the Bible, from Psalm 46: the God of peace stops wars, dismantles weapons, and is at work making peace. This is the God who made us, the God who calls us, the living God we will soon meet face to face. This God, it seems to me, is a God worth seeking and knowing, who is trying to disarm us through his loving nonviolence, even against our own collective wishes.

We don't hear much about this antiwar God these days. I doubt we ever did. I have often thought that the heart of our global crisis comes from our false image of God. Most of us imagine a god who makes war, blesses war, supports our wars, and admires our weapons. But this is not the God of Psalm 46 or the God of the nonviolent Jesus. In his Sermon on the Mount, Jesus names God as a peacemaker who practices universal nonviolent love toward all creation by letting the sun shine on the good and the bad and the rain fall on the just and the unjust. This true image of a nonviolent God changes everything. If God practices universal nonviolent love, then God has to do everything God can, within the boundaries of granting us free will, to stop our wars and dismantle our weapons.

～～～

As every spiritual director sees, God is always moving in close to us with love and blessings, and every individual responds positively up to a point—and then stops. Every one of us resists the movement of our peacemaking God at some point for some reason, usually because we are afraid of what might be asked of us, even though we may know that God only wants to love us and be with us like a doting parent. We don't realize that we are resisting God. That's why a spiritual director is so helpful. A good spiritual director is like a coach who sees God's movement toward us, and our movement away from God, and encourages us to go back to prayer and welcome God. If we knew and trusted God's total nonviolence, we would let God get close to us, rejoice in discovering the depth of God's peace and love, and allow our lives to be more peaceful, more loving, more nonviolent.

Few talk about our collective national and global resistance to God. And though collectively, nationally, even globally, we give God some small portion of name recognition, we certainly do not want to know God collectively, nationally, and globally and do what God might expect us to do—collectively, nationally, and globally.

Here, in Psalm 46 and elsewhere, we get a taste of God's attitude toward the nations and the world, which is to say, God's active distaste for war and weapons. Jesus will take this foundational understanding of God much further and announce that God is a God of peace, nonviolence, and love, and he will die trying to teach us the truth of nonviolence about the living God.

But this can't be, we grumble. If God is so peaceful, why doesn't God end our wars, dismantle our weapons, and make peace? Psalm 46 insists that the God of peace is in fact busy doing just that! You just won't hear about it on the evening news—or even in church on Sunday. The culture is dead set on maintaining war, power, and violence, and few anywhere, especially in the churches, want to rock the boat of war. So we go along believing the culture of war, its insistence that there's nothing we can do to change the world and its service of a false god of war.

~~~

"Come and see the works of God," the psalmist recommends. If you want to witness God's disarming action, get out of your comfort zone and go where the nonviolent action is. If you get involved with nonviolent people, with those serving the poor and advocating for justice, with those resisting war and building a global grassroots movement for the disarmament of the world, you will see the works of the God of peace all around you. If you set out on the journey "to see the works of the God of peace," I bet you will learn a surprising thing or two.

The God of peace is found on the margins, not in the center; on the edge, not in the axis of power; at the bottom, not at the top; among the least, not among the first; on the outskirts of empire, not in its headquarters. If we want to see God and God's work for peace, we have to go to the margins and the edges, and there we will find God at work disarming the world. In the process, we will learn something about faith and our lack of it, fear and the solution of love, peacemaking and the uselessness of warmaking.

Like many others, I have seen the God of peace at work to end war—in El Salvador, Iraq, Northern Ireland, the Philippines, Nicaragua, South Africa, Afghanistan, Colombia, Palestine, Mexico, Egypt, India—even here in the United States. Right in the darkest places of war, I have experienced the light of peace among amazing people building grassroots movements to resist injustice and promote positive social change.

When one studies the grassroots movements of peace and justice throughout history, one can trace the finger of God at work in the world. From the British Quakers who led the way for the abolition of slavery, to the suffragettes who demanded equality of women, through the Gandhian independence movement in India and the Kingian Civil Rights movement in the United States, to the countless other movements for positive social change, God is at work among us, leading us to resist evil and establish new cultures of peace. I see the God of peace behind the peaceful fall of the Berlin Wall and communism; the end of apartheid and the election of Nelson Mandela; the Singing revolution in Estonia and the Orange revolution in Ukraine; the people power movement in the Philippines and the Good Friday peace agreement in Northern Ireland; the Catonsville Nine anti-Vietnam War action and some three hundred other draft board raids that helped end the Vietnam War; the global grassroots movements to abolish landmines, cluster bombs, handgun violence, the death penalty, and nuclear weapons; and the growing global grassroots movement working for a Green New Deal and the end of fossil fuels and environmental destruction. I think these grassroots movements of nonviolence need to be taught as the work of God—from Jesus and his movement to Dr. King and his movement—as an incentive for each one of us to join God's grassroots movements at work today for disarmament and global economic, racial, and climate justice.

~~~

The journey of faith begins as we renounce violence and war and start the long pilgrimage of loving nonviolence and active peacemaking. Once we decide to reject violence and the culture of war, then questions about personal and common security arise. Who will protect us? How will we survive? What is the meaning of life? It's in that moment, relived every day in the life of the peacemaker, when we sincerely call upon God for help and protection. That's the moment too when we start sounding like the psalmist: God is our rock, our refuge, our shield, our strength, our ever-present help, we say. We nonviolent people need God; violent people don't. They rely on their violence and weapons; we rely solely on the God of peace.

"The God of peace is our refuge and our strength, an ever-present help in trouble," Psalm 46 begins. Even if the earth shakes, the mountains quake, the oceans rage, and the skies storm—the God of peace is with us, so we choose not to be afraid. That's a mighty promise, a powerful faith, and a good way to proceed through these dark times of right-wing politics, rampant racism, permanent warfare, rising fascism, economic collapse, and catastrophic climate change.

∿

Psalm 46 tells of the God who "stops wars to the ends of the earth, breaks the war bow, splinters the war spear, and burns the shields with fire." Who ever heard of such a God? What preacher ever characterizes God as the ultimate antiwar, antimilitary force in the universe? Psalm 46 claims that God breaks and destroys the instruments of mass murder. Do we believe this? More, do we want this kind of God?

If God was at work destroying the war bows, spears, and shields, what must God think and do about our nuclear weapons, F-15 fighter bombers, Trident submarines, smart bombs, Star Wars programs, and other systems of mass murder? Following the logic of the psalm, we can conclude that today the God of peace is actively working to break and destroy every single weapon in our arsenal. Following that logic, as servants of the God of peace, that means that God must not want us to join or support any military but to join and pursue this holy work of disarmament.

Psalm 46 calls us to join the global grassroots movement of peace and nonviolence. If we recite this psalm and worship this God, then we too have to learn our part to help end war, dismantle weapons, support new cultures of peace and nonviolence, and see the finger of God in the global grassroots movement for justice and peace.

～～

In the end, Psalm 46 issues one of God's great commandments: *"Be still and know that I am the God of peace."* This is how we become human: by entering the stillness and peace of the God of peace and knowing that God is the God of peace. If this is the one required thing, it is the one thing nearly every one of us avoids, and that is the reason the world is such a mess. We refuse to be still in the presence of God and know our God as the God of peace.

But it is never too late to start again. And so we are invited to sit in peace and quiet, to enter the holy stillness, to rest our minds and hearts and bodies, and there, in that peace and quiet, to know that God is the God of peace. We imagine we are in the presence of God, and so we enter God's peace and quiet. The invitation is to stay there, not to get up quickly, give up quickly, or move on quickly.

Sit still in God's presence and remain in that stillness. If this can become a daily practice, our normal rhythm, we may eventually awaken to the truth that the God of peace is God, that God really does want us to beat our swords into plowshares and study war no more, that God summons us to get involved in building a new culture of nonviolence, justice, and peace. We have our work cut out for us, but the burden is easy, because we get to be still and know that God is God.

7 Some Rely on Weapons; We Rely on the God of Peace ❋ PSALM 20

Some rely on chariots, others on horses,
but we rely on the name of the God of peace.
They will collapse and fall, but we will stand strong and firm.

There's an outrageous scene in the crazy 1970s comedy *Monty Python and the Holy Grail* when the troop pretends to be King Arthur and his knights losing a battle with a fearsome killer bunny. Feeling desperate, they call for the "Holy Hand Grenade of Antioch." They take it out of a big gold case, break into Latin chants, and incense it. Then they read from "the Holy Book of Armaments, chapter two, verses 9–21." In their most pompous British accents, the bishop and acolyte recite the prayer of Saint Attila as he raised the Holy Hand Grenade on high: "O Lord, bless this Thy holy hand grenade that with it Thou mayest blow Thine enemies to tiny bits, in thy Mercy."

It's wickedly funny—and spot on true. This is what church people have done for 1,700 years—asked God to bless their wars, their troops, and their weapons. This prayer for war, satirized by Monty Python, shows how little we understand God, how little faith we have in God, how little love we share, how far we have strayed from gospel nonviolence. Asking God to kill our enemies is, in the eyes of the nonviolent Jesus, blasphemy. For Jesus, God is the God of peace, and we are God's beloved sons and daughters; and so we too are peacemakers. As we come to know and understand God, we recognize that God is universal love—therefore total nonviolence—and can have nothing to do with war, except work to stop it. The journey of faith begins when we recognize that the living God blesses only peace and universal love. Anything else is blasphemy.

Psalm 20 is an ancient prayer of blasphemy, like every prayer for war recited over the past few thousand years. It's the hapless cry: "God bless our troops!" Saying such words betrays the truth that we know next to nothing about the living God of peace. If anything, God curses our troops—and every military and war throughout history, including our own wars today. Violence in response to violence only leads to further violence; God, on the other hand, practices infinite holy nonviolence and works to overcome violence through active divine nonviolence.

In this case, Psalm 20 calls for God to bless the king as he leads the troops into battle to kill all the horrible enemy soldiers. If God is a perfectly loving, infinitely nonviolent, generous parent to every human being who ever existed, why would God ever want to kill anyone? God wouldn't! God loves every human being fully and wants every human being to reach the fullness of a nonviolent life.

As the psalm prays for victory in battle, we read:

> Some rely on chariots, others on horses,
> but we rely on the name of the God of peace.
> They will collapse and fall, but we will stand strong and firm.

If we read these verses from the perspective of gospel nonviolence, as Jesus would have, then we discover a new kind of wisdom—the faith that comes with nonviolence. Read from the perspective of nonviolence, the psalms can strengthen our faith in the God of peace and help us to reject the weapons of war and violence around us and instead stand strong and firm as nonviolent people. It's like the whole human race is addicted to violence and war, but some few of us want to become sober people of nonviolence and peace. We renounce violence, turn to our higher power, help one another in communities of peace, and try to live from now on within the boundaries of nonviolence. Through this "Violence Anonymous" model of the church, we can stand strong and firm as nonviolent followers of the nonviolent Jesus.

Incidentally, in this psalm, when we pray for "victory," the Hebrew word for "victory" can also mean "salvation." From a perspective of nonviolence, then, we pray for victory over violence and war, for salvation from our addiction to violence and war. Salvation in this light means the sobriety of peace that the nonviolent Jesus offers to us.

If we are going to rely on the God of peace, then we have to learn that we have to seek peace and pursue it, that the means of peace are the only way to the God of peace, and that the days of war are coming to an end. Starting with us, we are going to rewrite the Scriptures and disarm the church and discover the boundaries of nonviolence that make an active faith in the God of peace viable. That's the journey and the prayer of the peacemaker.

8 "Their Idols Are Silver and Gold"
PSALM 115

Their idols are silver and gold, the work of human hands.
They have mouths but do not speak; eyes, but do not see.
They have ears, but do not hear; noses, but do not smell.
They have hands, but do not feel; feet, but do not walk;
and no sound rises from their throats.
Their makers shall be like them, all who trust in them.

Psalm 115 may not seem like a psalm of peace, but for me, it gets right to the heart of the matter. Peacemaking requires faith and trust in the living God of peace, as opposed to faith and trust in the culture of war and its idols of death. The idols are dead, and so are those who worship them. In other words, you can't live in peace and the fullness of life if you spend your years serving war and the idols of death.

"The great sin, the source of all other sin, is idolatry and never has it been greater, more prevalent, than now," Thomas Merton wrote on Good Friday a few months before his death in 1968.

> Yet it is almost completely unrecognized precisely because it is so overwhelming and so total. It takes in everything. There is nothing else left. Fetishism of power, machines, possessions, medicines, sports, clothes, etc., all kept going by greed for money and power. The bomb is only one accidental aspect of the cult....We should be thankful for it as a sign, a revelation of what all the rest of our civilization points to. The self-immolation of humanity to its own greed and its own despair. And behind it all are the principalities and powers whom humanity serves in this idolatry.

When I was younger, I didn't understand idolatry and would have thought this psalm only poetry. But for three decades I heard my friends Daniel and Philip Berrigan reflect on Psalm 115 as a clear denunciation of the weapons of mass destruction in which we place our security. Their sharp words surprised and unsettled me. I went to them expecting to hear reflections on peace and heard instead condemnation of the idols of war. It has taken me a long time to understand what they were teaching.

Like their friend Thomas Merton, the Berrigans testified to their faith in the living God of peace, but they insisted that such faith needs boundaries. Belief in the God of peace, in a culture as sick as ours, requires publicly renouncing belief in the culture's false gods of war—the idols of nuclear weapons, Trident submarines, drones, AK-47s, and all other instruments of killing. In other words, as we name our faith in the God of peace, we likewise have to denounce the culture's faith in the idols of war, as Psalm 115 does. We have to do both if we want to live in peace and the fullness of life.

Like most people, I have lived my whole life in the shadow of the atomic bomb. I have never known a nuclear-free world. I grew up during the Vietnam War, and later took active part in opposing all US wars in Central America, Iraq, Afghanistan, Syria, and elsewhere. All my life, I never forgot that the doomsday clock was ticking, that our arsenal could extinguish millions of people at any minute. I recognized the bomb as the ultimate idol of death. It is antilife, antihumanity, anti-earth, anti-Christ, anti-God. Yet despite its horrific potential to kill and destroy, we continue to pay for them, maintain them, and build them. As Merton comments, they are the ultimate sign of our sickness; I would add: of our social insanity.

"I hold that those who invented the atomic bomb have committed the gravest sin," Mahatma Gandhi said shortly after the United States dropped the atomic bomb on Hiroshima and Nagasaki in August 1945. "The atomic bomb brought an empty victory to the Allied arms, but it resulted for the time being in destroying Japan. What has happened to the soul of the destroying nation is yet too early to see."

For nearly twenty years, while living in New Mexico near Los Alamos, the birthplace of the atomic bomb, I led an annual peace vigil to commemorate the Hiroshima and Nagasaki anniversaries and denounce the big business of the US nuclear weapons industry. I consider the National Labs in Los Alamos to be the greatest center of idolatry on the planet and in the history of the world. While New Mexico remains one of the poorest states in the United States, its politicians continue to defend the bomb and spend billions on the bomb, when those funds are needed for food, housing, health care, education, jobs, and dignity for its impoverished people. Everyone is under the spell of the bomb.

How do we address and change this mad waste of funds that poisons the land, bankrupts the nation, and cannot protect us in the least?

Gandhi said you need to teach nonviolence, engage in public non-cooperation, and use symbols. My friends and I decided one year to sit in sackcloth and ashes as a symbolic way to beg God's forgiveness and ask for the grace of disarmament. We would sit quietly for thirty minutes, sometimes hundreds of us, then march to the park where the original atomic bomb was built and hold rallies and teach-ins for disarmament. It was always peaceful, but it sparked a nerve.

One year, the local Catholic pastor wrote a lead editorial in the state newspaper condemning me for keeping vigil for peace at Los Alamos and insisting that the church was against nuclear weapons. In response, the archbishop called me in, forbade me from praying publicly for peace, and told me that God can't protect us, only our nuclear weapons can. Eventually he removed my priestly faculties giving me permission to say Mass, and I left the state. No priest in US history, including Thomas Merton and Daniel Berrigan, was ever punished for their public stand for peace the way I was. I was treated worse than the pedophile priests. It seemed every Catholic and Christian in the state agreed with the archbishop: God blesses our nuclear weapons.

Reflecting on these experiences, I conclude that Gandhi's prediction has come true. These days, we see the effects of the nuclear bomb upon us—from the trillions wasted on these useless weapons to the collapse of our economy and social infrastructure; from our willing destruction of the environment, our addiction to war, and our corporate greed to our presidential approval of weapons of mass destruction; from the fall-out of violence everywhere, including rampant racism and the insane mass shootings in high schools, concerts, churches, and gay clubs, to the senseless global hunger and extreme poverty around the world.

Underneath this social collapse and epidemic of violence is the loss of meaning, truth, faith, spirituality, and basic humanity. As Gandhi suspected, we have become soulless. We have become as dead as the metallic weapons we have created. We created these idols of death—

in effect, worshiped these idols of death—and then become as dead as these idols of death. Like our weapons, we have mouths but do not speak for peace, eyes but do not see the vision of peace, ears but do not hear the good news of peace, hands but do not reach out in peace, feet but do not walk the road to peace. The psalmist was right.

"The nuclear bomb is the most antidemocratic, antinational, anti-human, outright evil thing that humans have ever made," my friend Arundhati Roy writes. "If you are religious, then remember that this bomb is humanity's challenge to God. It's worded quite simply: 'We have the power to destroy everything that You have created.' If you're not religious," she continues, "then look at it this way. This world of ours is four thousand, six hundred million years old. It could end in an afternoon."

〜

The only way spiritually to reclaim our soul is to stop making these nuclear weapons and start practicing nonviolence as a whole new way of life. We all need to join and support the global grassroots movements to push for their abolition and instead spend those billions on food for the hungry, homes for the homeless, health care, jobs, and education for everyone, and with the billions left over, teach everyone the methodology of nonviolent conflict resolution. As we take these common-sense steps toward peace, we will discover what faith in the living God of peace feels like and begin to come alive again.

〜

Psalm 115 begins with the taunt asked every peacemaker in history: Where is your God? Why do you obey God's way of nonviolence? How can this God of peace protect you?

"Our God is in heaven," the psalmist answers calmly, "and does whatever God wants to do." The psalmist then proceeds to deconstruct the culture's false gods as empty, lifeless shells and saves the punch line for last: those who make these idols become as empty and lifeless as the idols themselves!

Those who build and maintain weapons of war, greed, and violence, Psalm 115 declares, become like these idols. Those who make peace and serve the living God of peace, on the other hand, become the sons and daughters of the God of peace.

Is this too harsh? The language of the psalms can be harsh, and the question of idolatry is one that no one likes to face. We prefer to avoid these big topics and live in denial. As Merton writes, idolatry has reached unparalleled heights. We don't even realize that we're idolaters. Idolatry has become the new norm, our ordinary spirituality.

Recently the Pentagon announced that its new 30,000-pound bunker-buster "Superbomb" was "ready for use." "The biggest conventional bomb ever developed is ready!" the spokesperson said gleefully. The Pentagon has spent $330 million to develop and deliver more than twenty of these precision-guided Massive Ordnance Penetrator bunker-busters, which are designed to blast through more than two hundred feet of concrete.

"They have mouths but do not speak, ears but do not hear....Their makers shall be like them, all who trust in them."

The psalmist names the idols as inhuman and ungodly and the idolaters as inhuman and ungodly too. We need to name the idols of today as inhuman and ungodly and help each other resist the culture's idolatry so that we can become more human and more Godly.

We think, incorrectly, that we can have both God and nukes, God and money, God and Wall Street, God and empire, God and war. The psalmist and the evangelists insist that it's one or the other. God does not allow for other false gods. The minute we give in to our worship of these false gods, we reject the living God of peace. Then we start down the path of spiritual death.

Dan and Phil Berrigan taught me that the best way toward the fullness of life, toward God, is by our nonviolent resistance to the idols of death. That's why many of us commemorate Hiroshima every year, to say no to the idolatry of nuclear weapons and yes to the possibilities of life. Our resistance helps us exercise our faith. It leads us to understand anew what faith in the God of peace means.

Dan and Phil put it like this: "Don't worship the idols of death! Know where you stand. Be clear about whom you worship and what you do not worship. If you worship the living God of peace, then do not also worship the false gods of money and power, the idols of war and death. Take your life and faith seriously. Understand the social, global implications of faith. Remember that life is short and do your part to help humanity reclaim the gift of peace."

Psalm 115 is a prayer of hope and trust in our quiet, gentle God of peace who does not violently intervene, who mourns our common disbelief and idolatry, and who blesses our small peacemaking efforts, even though we might see few tangible results.

"Not to us, God of peace, not to us, but to your name give glory because of your faithfulness and love," we read. For the psalmist and the rest of us, our main focus becomes the God of peace. God is the one who is faithful and loving, not us. As we try to remain faithful to the God of peace, we will be blessed with peace.

"May you be blessed by the God of peace who made heaven and earth," the psalmist concludes. That is the hope and prayer of the psalms of peace, of all peacemakers. As we reject the idols of war and death, choose to be people of faith and trust, look to the God of peace, and practice God's way of nonviolence, we know we will receive the blessing reserved for peacemakers.

9 The God of Peace Takes No Delight in the Strength of the War Horse
PSALM 147

"The God of peace takes no delight in the strength of the war horse, no pleasure in the stride of the warrior," we read in Psalm 147. "Rather, the God of peace takes pleasure in those who fear him, in those who hope in his steadfast love."

Here again we are presented with a basic truth: God despises our wars, weapons, and violence and much prefers our hope and trust in his gentleness and mercy. I translate that to mean that God is a God of nonviolence and looks for people of nonviolence to be with him. That means we're called to become like God, people of active, creative gentleness, mercy, and nonviolence.

To that end, we're given a series of descriptions about this kind, generous God: God heals the brokenhearted, binds up the wounds of the injured, gathers those who have had to flee, helps the poor, permits the rain to fall and the grass to grow, feeds the animals, and even provides for the birds. This is a lavish God, one worthy of our hope and trust. This is a God worth believing in.

Those who trust and hope in the God of peace, we're told, will have children who are blessed, will receive the finest wheat, and will welcome peace in their land. Because of these blessings, they go forth to sing God's praise, give thanks to God, and glorify God. It's a beautiful testimony to the gentle nature of God and an invitation to trust and hope in this gentle, merciful, nonviolent God, come what may.

This is our destiny, I hear the psalm announce—to hope and trust in the God of peace, to welcome God's peace, and to sing and glorify the God of peace. This is what God is looking for from us. What's not to like? Let's get with the program!

When I look around at the beauty of creation, the beauty of humanity, the beauty of every single person, I turn to the Creator with wonder and awe and give thanks and praise. I hope this is the normal, natural future for each one of us, if we only let go and trust—to spend our days thanking the One who made us as we learn to live God's way of peace and generous love.

If this is the general plan for all life, then we do not want to waste another second hurting another person, supporting war or corporate greed, enabling racism or sexism or poverty, or destroying Mother Earth. Anything less than hope and trust in the God of peace, and our own peacemaking lives, insults God. We do not want to mock God. We want to please the God of peace. All we have to do is try, and we're already there.

This reminds me of the old spiritual, folk song, protest song, "Ain't Gonna Study War No More." I've been singing it at protests with my friends for many decades. My favorite version is a joint recording made in the mid-1950s by Elvis Presley, Johnny Cash, Carl Perkins, and Jerry Lee Lewis at the Sun Studios in Memphis. With these big stars, the hymn becomes a mantra, a new translation of an ancient psalm:

> *I'm gonna lay down my sword and shield*
> *Down by the riverside, down by the riverside, down by the riverside.*
> *I'm gonna lay down my sword and shield*
> *Down by the riverside. Gonna study war no more*
> *I ain't gonna study war no more, ain't gonna study war no more,*
> *I ain't gonna study war no more. I ain't gonna study war no more,*
> *I ain't gonna study war no more, I ain't gonna study war no more.*

The God of peace calls us to the life of peace, and the more we can embrace this spiritual vision and reject the world's insane violence, the more we praise the God of peace and give thanks for such a beautiful

God and such a beautiful future. At that moment, we realize the psalm-ist is right, and we join with the chorus:

> *How good it is to sing praises to our God!*
> *How pleasant to give fitting praise!...*
> *Great is our God, vast in power,*
> *with understanding beyond measure....*
> *Offer praise to your God!*

III

The Beauty of Peace

THE CELEBRATION OF THE PEACEMAKER

Let the heavens be glad; let the earth rejoice;
let the sea roar and what fills it resound;
let the fields be joyful and all that is in them.
Then let all the trees of the forest rejoice
before the God of peace who comes,
who comes to govern the earth,
to govern the world with justice and the
peoples with faithfulness.

PSALM 96

10 **Awesome!** ❋ PSALM 8

Along the Central Coast of California where I live, there's a ten-mile strand of beach just north of the towering rock at Morro Bay that attracts a steady stream of sandpipers, pelicans, cormorants, sanderlings, gulls, seals, terns, and tourists. The Morro Bay rock stands 581 feet tall, a stunning beautiful mass right in the harbor that you can't take your eyes off. It's hypnotic, mesmerizing, perhaps the most beautiful natural site on the west coast of North America.

Along its south side rests the harbor around the village, and in that quiet waterway lies a group of sea otters floating on their backs, eating kelp, and tending to their young. These adorable creatures are like puppy dogs. Sometimes, you see them with a rock on their chest, breaking clams open to eat. Other times they appear to be sleeping on their backs. They look at us as much as we look at them. Happily, their existence is a rare success story. A hundred years ago, we nearly killed them to extinction, with literally only fifty left. Today there are over two thousand along the coast.

It's a clear blue day as I walk along the beach, taking in the brisk air, pondering the massive rock, listening to the crashing waves, studying the coastline north to see the spot where I live. Along the breaking waves, strange exotic brown birds with long skinny legs and long bills or beaks curving down from their mouths walk in the shallow water in groups of twenty or so. These are the Long-billed Curlews. Their beaks can be ten inches long. They are not to be confused with the Marbled Godwits, who have shorter beaks. They peck at the sand, looking for food, and eventually fly off farther down the strand when a dog runs toward them barking. In such moments, in the innocence, freshness, and wonder of life, I feel grateful to be alive.

Farther north, on the road to Big Sur, just past Cambria, hundreds of giant elephant seals sleep on the sand for months at a time. Tourists gather along the cliff fence above staring down at them, taking in this spectacle. These creatures are massive piles of moving blubber who can swim far out at sea for months. They need this long period of rest to survive. Some snore; some fight with one another. Some try to crawl back into the ocean; others crawl along for a better spot. Others bark; the pups cry out. What was God thinking when he made them, I ask myself. Maybe God uses these massive creatures to teach us humans the importance of peace, quiet, and a good rest. Everyone is spellbound looking down at the hundreds of these creatures lying on the sand. They too invite wonder and thanksgiving.

Here on the Central Coast it's easy to get lost in the beauty of creation, to spend hours mesmerized by such creatures, the rolling sea, the cliffs, the birds, and, on occasion, the distant whales. I find myself saying involuntarily, "Wow, thank you God!" I bless them, take a deep breath, notice how fresh and alive the coast makes me feel, and find myself strengthened for the work of justice and peace. Here, it's contemplation made easy.

~~~

Perhaps the best feature of the psalms is their celebration of creation and all creatures, and therefore the Creator. While there are many lamentations, these outbursts of joy over the splendor of creation and the wonder of the Creator are especially helpful in these days of catastrophic climate change. These psalms remind us that the Creator has given us a great gift—Mother Earth and her creatures. These psalms help us to remember, which is important, because clearly we have forgotten.

After centuries of systemic greed and violence, of digging up fossil fuels, we have raised earth's temperature and unleashed catastrophic climate change. In this climate chaos, we will suffer through droughts, fires, hurricanes, tornadoes, rain bombs, floods, mudslides, and terrible winds. As the temperature rises, the polar ice caps melt, and the sea levels rise. Hundreds of millions of people will have to flee and fight over land and water. It's a grim future of countless new wars, starvation, and disease on a much-less-livable planet.

The path forward requires a global grassroots movement of nonviolence, the likes of which the world has never seen, to create global political will, to set the world on the path of renewable energy, and to help us all reconnect with creation. If we are going to learn the wisdom of nonviolence, we have to reconnect with Mother Earth and her creatures, live in right relationship as the Creator intended us to live, and begin to practice nonviolence toward one another so that we can create new cultures of nonviolence.

These creation psalms remind us of our place in the grand scheme of things. They can inspire us to make peace with Mother Earth, to celebrate earth and sky, sun and moon, the oceans and mountains, the birds and fish and all the wondrous creatures. They can take us back to the basics of childlike wonder in this Garden of Eden God has given us. As we celebrate creation with the psalmist, and give thanks to the Creator for this generous gift, our hearts can fill with wonder and praise.

We need that wonder and praise if we are going to take seriously the reality of climate change and the need for grassroots political action. As we reconnect with Mother Earth and do our part to stop its destruction, we will reconnect with one another and the Creator and, through these psalms, find a positive spirit to keep us going. They can help us rediscover our rightful place in creation among God's creatures and live at one with creation. In other words, I think they can help us on our journey of nonviolence toward universal peace.

"God of peace, how awesome is your name through all the earth!" we read in Psalm 8. "I sing of your majesty. When I look at your heavens, the work of your fingers, the moon and stars that you set in place—I ask, 'Who are human beings that you are mindful of us? Who am I that you would care for me?' You have crowned us with glory and honor, allowed us to rule over the works of your hands. You have put all things at our feet, given us stewardship for all creatures, from the sheep and oxen to the birds of the air and the fish of the sea. For this, we thank you, we bless you and we praise you!" Amen.

11 Brother Sun, Sister Moon
PSALM 104

When you step out of the Basilica of St. Francis, in Assisi, Italy, and walk across the lawn, and turn right, down the mountain into the fields, you enter into the wilds of nature that stirred Francis to the heights of praise. It's June 2019, and I'm here for ten days to lead a peace pilgrimage through Assisi for Pace e Bene, the peace group I work with. Thirty-five of us are visiting the holy shrines, enjoying lectures on the Franciscan teachings of peace, praying at Mass at the holy sites, and spending the week together on retreat. We're reflecting on the peacemaking lives of St. Francis and St. Clare to better understand the peacemaking life of Jesus and our own peacemaking journeys.

Assisi is the world's most mythic city of peace and nonviolence. Pilgrims journey there by the millions to feel a vibe of peace they've never felt before, a spirituality of peace that breathes through the landscape and the town into the pilgrim's heart.

On the first full day, we tour the Basilica of St. Francis, and near the tomb of St. Francis I preside at Mass and preach on gospel nonviolence. On the second day, we visit San Damiano, the little church built by hand by St. Francis himself. Here, long ago, he heard Jesus speak to him from the cross, and so I preached on hearing the call of Jesus and taking up the cross as the way of nonviolence in a world of violence. The cross that spoke to St. Francis still exists, and is now kept at the Basilica of St. Clare, which we visited the next day and where we had Mass right at the tomb of St. Clare. She and her monastic community of nuns moved into San Damiano, and she lived there for decades until her death.

Once, while Francis was visiting Clare at San Damiano, he sat in the garden, meditating on the wonders of creation, and wrote his beloved "Canticle of Creation." There he praises creation and the Creator for the glories of creation. It's one of the most inspiring writings of all time.

Francis' canticle offers a powerful antidote to the despair of today, to a new world of catastrophic climate change. Instead of giving up and doing nothing, Francis invites us to notice creation, celebrate creation, find the Creator through creation, and in that celebration, find new strength to live at one in peace with Mother Earth and all humanity. Here is my translation of St. Francis' canticle. I offer it as a way for us to notice the wonders of creation, to reconnect with creation and the Creator, and to praise God:

> *Most High, all-powerful, all-good God of peace,*
> *all praise is Yours, all glory, all honor, and all blessings.*
> *To you alone, Most High, do they belong, and*
> *no mortal lips are worthy to pronounce Your Name.*
>
> *Praised be You, God of peace, with all Your creatures,*
> *especially Brother Sun, who is the day through whom You give us light.*
> *He is beautiful and radiant with great splendor; of You Most High,*
> *   he bears the likeness.*
>
> *Praised be You, my Lord, through Sister Moon and the stars, in the*
> *   heavens you have made them bright, precious, and fair.*
>
> *Praised be You, my Lord, through Brothers Wind and Air, and fair*

*and stormy, all weather's moods, by which You cherish all that
You have made.*

*Praised be You, my Lord, through Sister Water, so useful, humble,
precious, and pure.*

*Praised be You, my Lord, through Brother Fire, through whom You
light the night and he is beautiful and playful and robust
and strong.*

*Praised be You, my Lord, through our Sister, Mother Earth,
who sustains and governs us,
producing varied fruits with colored flowers and herbs.*

*Praise be You, my Lord, through those who grant pardon for love of
You and bear sickness and trial. Blessed are those who endure
in peace. By You, Most High, they will be crowned.*

*Praised be You, my Lord, through Sister Death, from whom no one
living can escape. Blessed are they She finds doing Your Will.*

*Praise and bless the God of peace and give God thanks. Let us
serve the God of peace with great humility, gentleness, and
nonviolence, all the days of our lives. Amen.*

Like St. Francis, we celebrate the wonders of creation and learn anew to
serve creation and humanity and praise the Creator. This prayer helps
us to see the finger of God everywhere around us—in the sun and the
moon, the ocean and the mountains, the trees and the meadows, the
birds and the animals. As we give new thanks to God, we can begin
again to make peace with Mother Earth, all creatures, and all humani-

ty. As we reconnect with Mother Earth, we rediscover the meaning of life—our call to be peacemakers.

~~~

My guess is that St. Francis felt inspired to write this hymn through his reading of the psalms, in particular Psalm 104. This psalm celebrates God's handiwork in creation as a pathway to peace. It reminds us that we are one with creation, that the Creator has given us this beautiful earth as a gift of peace, and that we are called to make peace with creation, not destroy it. It begins with over-the-top praise for the God of peace, describing the Creator astride creation:

> *God of peace, you are great indeed!*
> *You are clothed with majesty and splendor, robed in light.*
> *You stretch out the heavens like a tent....*
> *You make the clouds your chariot;*
> *riding on the wings of the wind.*
> *You make the winds your messengers;*
> *flaming fire are your ministers.*

I like the image of God as light, riding on the clouds, traveling through the winds, and sending fire as his minister. For me, God is the spirit of unconditional, nonviolent, universal love, the force of Love wildly in love with every human being, every creature, and all creation. The psalms and gospels invite us to enter that wild universal love, to feel it, catch it, pursue it, and join it forever and so become instruments of that same wild, nonviolent universal love. As we do, we too become light and ride on the clouds and travel through the winds. Amen.

~~~

Then, the psalmist describes how God created Mother Earth and all the creatures:

> *You set the earth on its foundation, so it can never be shaken.*
> *Above the mountains stood the waters. At the sound of your thunder*
> *they fled.*
> *They rushed up to the mountains, ran down to the valleys*
> *to the place you had fixed for them.*
> *You made springs flow in the valleys that wind*
> *among the mountains.*
> *They give drink to every animal of the field;*
> *here wild asses quench their thirst.*
> *Beside them the birds of heaven nest;*
> *they sing among the branches.*
> *You water the mountains from your lofty abode;*
> *from the fruit of your labor the earth abounds.*
> *You make the grass grow for the cattle and plants*
> *for people's work*
> *to bring forth food from the earth, and wine to gladden*
> *their hearts,*
> *oil to make their faces shine, and bread to strengthen*
> *the human heart.*
> *The trees drink their fill, the cedars of Lebanon,*
> *which you planted.*
> *In them the birds build their nests; the stork in the junipers,*
> *its home.*
> *The high mountains are for the wild goats; the rocky cliffs,*
> *a refuge for badgers.*
> *You made the moon to mark the seasons, the sun that knows the*
> *hour of its setting.*

You make darkness and night falls, when all the animals of the forest
  wander about.
Young lions roar for prey, seeking their food from God.
When the sun rises, they steal away and settle down in their dens.
People go out to their work and to their labor till evening falls.

This hymn covers the basics of God's handiwork and reminds us to
notice these basics, to celebrate them, to find God in them, and to
honor them: Mother Earth herself, the mountains, the waters, the sun,
the moon, the rain, the thunder, the darkness, the night, the trees, valleys, springs, animals, cattle, birds, wild goats, badgers, lions, grasses,
plants, and food from the earth for people. Note especially the kindness
of God: "wine to gladden their hearts," bread "to sustain the human
heart." I like to savor the gifts of creation, to look closely at nature, to
let nature heal me and feed me and sustain me and gladden me. The
more we can enter mindfulness into the present moment of the creation around us, the more we too will celebrate and be glad.

This contemplative practice over the wonders of creation leads easily
to a new round of praise for the variety of God's wondrous creation:

How varied are your works, God of peace.
In wisdom you have made them all; the earth
  is full of your creatures.
There is the sea, great and wide! It teems with countless beings,
living things both large and small.
There go the ships, and Leviathan, whom you formed to play
  in the deep.
All of these look to you to give them food in due time.
When you give it to them, they gather; when you open your hand,
  they are filled with good things.

When you send forth your spirit, they are created, and you renew the
face of the earth.

You did all this, God, we proclaim. You made all this glory. We can add:
we have forgotten it, grown apart, become disconnected, but now, we
want to return to the Garden, to rediscover our roots, to be grounded
once again, and to recognize your creation as your handiwork, as your
gift of love for us. We want to be with you, God of peace.

This realization leads to a final hymn of praise, promise, and hope:

May the glory of the God of peace endure forever.
May the God of peace be glad in these works!
I will rejoice in the God of peace.
I will sing to the God of peace all my life.
I will sing praise to my God while I live.
May my meditation be pleasing to the God of peace.

What a perfect closing prayer: "May your glory endure forever; may
you be glad because of all your glorious creation. Then, I will always
rejoice in the God of peace; I will always sing to the God of peace; I will
praise God every day as long as I live!"

And then the conclusion: "May my daily meditation be pleasing to
the God of peace!" What an invitation. The point of our meditation
is not to please ourselves but to please the God of peace! Even in our
prayer, we have to get out of ourselves, get over our narcissism, focus
entirely on the God of peace, and always try to please the God of peace.
That, the psalmist teaches, is the point of life. May it be so always!

12 The Earth Is God's

PSALM 24

I 'm walking along the cliff about twenty feet above the crashing waves below, right on Highway One, where I live on the road to Big Sur along the Central Coast of California. The ocean is rough today, but the sun is out, and there's a cool breeze. Seagulls glide along the cliff, where white egrets keep watch in the fields; yellow and orange wildflowers grow here and there; cormorants and pelicans sit on the large rocks out in the water as I search the horizon for whales.

I have stepped into another world—the real world of creation, not the false illusion of Trump's America, Hollywood, Wall Street, Fox News, and the White House, but the exquisite beauty of ocean, sky, and mountains. My heart opens wide as I breathe in the fresh air and welcome Mother Earth's beauty. I can't help myself. I look up and say, "Thank you. I praise you for this natural beauty. You have outdone yourself. As long as I'm alive, I will praise you for this wondrous creation."

This is the new normal for me. As I turn sixty, I face the world of war, poverty, racism, nuclear weapons, and environmental destruction and, at the same time, turn closer to the wild world of creation, in my case, the central coast of California. There I find God's fingerprints at every turn. There I walk and breathe and feel at peace and give thanks and praise to the Creator. I try to walk this coast every day, and when I do, the world's bad news falls away, and the truth of reality, the beauty of the Creator, creation, humanity, and my own poor soul become one again and I realize the fullness of life and peace.

These walks, this scenery, this spectacular ocean coast, this fresh air is so far greater than anything on TV, any press release from the warmaking media, any pronouncement from the White House, any image from Hollywood, any media hype or cultural phenomenon. The reality of creation is so real, so astonishing, so grand, that as you step into it you become one with it, and then one with the God of peace. It is, hands down, the only real experience. You are one with creation and, thus, one with the Creator, as we strive to live at one with suffering humanity. Isn't that the point of life?

I walk these steps intentionally, mindfully, one moment at a time, in order to seek peace and pursue it, and I find that I have stepped into peace. With each step, I become one with creation, one with the Creator, one with humanity and the creatures. With each step, I try to represent humanity, to reconnect with creation, to live as we were all intended to live. It might seem silly or useless or pointless, but the mystical dimensions tell me otherwise. I know now there's a connection, and why not? The earth does not belong to us. It belongs to God. As we appreciate Mother Earth, we appreciate the One who made her and gave her to us.

That's what we hear in the mystical teachings of Psalm 24: the earth belongs to God, and so do we, and it's time to wake up and give ourselves to this loving, beautiful God. And so we read:

> *The earth is God's and all it holds,*
> *the world and those who live in it.*
> *For God founded it on the seas,*
> *and established it on the rivers.*
>
> *Who may go up the mountain of the God of peace?*
> *Who can stand in God's holy place?*
>
> *"The clean of hand and pure of heart,*
> *those who have not given their souls to useless things,*
> *to what is vain.*
> *They will receive blessings from the God of peace*
> *and justice from a saving God.*

Such are the ones who seek God,
who seek the face of the God of Jacob."

Who climbs God's holy mountain? Who stands in God's holy place? Who becomes one with creation and therefore with the Creator? The psalmist tells us: those who are clean of hand and pure of heart; those who do not waste their time with useless things (like money, possessions, and ego). They will receive blessings and justice from the God of peace.

Clean of hand and pure of heart. Here's a phrase we can pursue for life. I translate it to mean: there is no blood on our hands. There is no violence in our hearts. Our hands are not used to hit people, hurt people, point at and bully people, hold guns, build nuclear weapons, or push the button to drop bombs. Our hearts are not centers of violence, anger, jealousy, rage, resentment, bitterness, revenge, retaliation, and war.

Because we are addicted to violence and raised in a culture of violence, the psalmist calls us to a new journey of nonviolence so that we might be one with God's creation—that we have nonviolent hands and nonviolent hearts. In our journey into nature, we enter the disarmament of our hands and hearts, our minds and bodies, so that we become true peacemakers who live at peace with God's peaceful creation. Only on this path of disarmament and nonviolence will we be given blessings of peace from the God of peace.

The spiritual life, then, is a journey toward disarmed hands, disarmed hearts, and disarmed lives, that we might live in the peace of the God of peace. No more violence, no more cooperation with the culture of violence, no more inner violence mimicking the world's violence. Instead, we live and breathe in peace, cultivate loving-kindness and compassion, enjoy gentleness in every aspect of our lives, and find there a new strength we hadn't previously known, the strength of peace that springs from oneness with creation. This new journey will lead us one day to see the face of the God of peace, to a joy we have never known.

13 The Heavens Declare the Glory of God ☀ PSALM 19

The heavens declare the glory of the God of peace.
The sky proclaims its builder's craft....
The law of the Lord is perfect, reviving the soul.
The decrees of the Lord are trustworthy, giving wisdom
    to the simple.
The precepts of the Lord are right, rejoicing the heart.
The command of the Lord is clear, enlightening the eyes.
The fear of the Lord is pure, enduring forever.
The statutes of the Lord are true, all of them just.
More to be desired than fine gold.

Sometimes, the summer sunsets over my New Mexico mesa set off a sky of swirling colors—yellow, blue, red, and orange—that were greater than any Van Gogh or Picasso painting, greater than an LSD trip or Hollywood CGI. I would sit on my little porch in a rocker stunned, taking it all in, watching it in detail, and thanking God. It seemed like I was the only person on earth aware of this majestic skyscape and that it was done for me alone. Year after year, I spent my summer evenings watching those spectacular sunsets. Every night, I saw the glory of the Creator. Sometimes I would say to God, "That was your best work." Other times, "Now you're just showing off!"

Everything in the sky points to a generous Creator, who built a place of wonder for us to dwell. If creation is so gorgeous, so spectacular, so marvelous to behold, how much more so the Creator? That's the logic of Psalm 19 that I find appealing. "The glory of God, the builder's craft." When I walk along the ocean, or the edge of the Grand Canyon, or Yosemite's Valley floor, or the New Mexico high desert, or on the cliff edge of the Aran Islands off to the west of Ireland, or along a sandy Hawaiian beach, I am gobsmacked by the builder's craft. The hail storms, blizzards, meteor showers, rainbows, thunderstorms—these raise the bar even higher. If you are attuned to nature, and live close to it, then you notice its power and every changing wonder and feel the presence of God all around you. Perhaps this is a peculiar grace, but I think it's available to everyone if you seek out oneness with creation. Since I was a child, I've easily found God's fingerprints in these natural marvels and given thanks in childlike wonder. No matter how bad the news of the world, the heavens declare the glory of God, and the gift of peace is still offered to those alive on earth.

The psalmist argues that everything the God of peace says and does is perfect. The law of the God of peace, the decrees of the God of peace, the precepts of the God of the peace, the commands of the God of peace, the fear (or awe) of the God of peace, the statutes of the God of peace—all are right, true, just, trustworthy, clear, enduring; all of them refresh, enlighten, endure, give wisdom, and cause rejoicing. The laws of God are laws of peace, love, compassion, justice, and nonviolence; they are glorious because the God of peace is glorious. They describe the way and life and wisdom of God and invite us more and more fully into the glory of God.

Sometimes at midnight in New Mexico, alone on the mesa at eight thousand feet, I would walk outside onto the desert to look up at the night sky. A million stars would appear in the summer sky. No, sometimes it looked like a billion. If you saw a picture of it or a piece of artwork like that, you wouldn't believe it. The pink Milky Way would run through the center of the sky. I saw this over and over again, over many years. It was so beautiful, so mysterious, it was hard to take in, and that's why, I decided, few people spend time studying that spectacle of the New Mexico night sky. It is too big, too unfathomable, too beautiful, and clearly points to a Creator. We are so small in comparison, our everyday worries and anxieties and concerns so ridiculous next to such glory. The glory of God, like the heavens itself, and God's laws of peace, I decided, are shy and humble and gentle. They will not force themselves upon you. If you are too busy, too stressed out, too angry, too mean, too addicted, too workaholic, you will miss it and so never believe the ever-present glory of God surrounding us.

In the end, it's a choice. We have to seek this truth. In other words, Psalm 19 instructs us: get up, go and see and hear the heavens declare the glory of the God of peace, discover the builder's craft, learn for yourself the enlightening, trustworthy, clear, enduring, refreshing, wise, true ways of God, and rejoice.

14 The Hope of All the Ends of the Earth
PSALM 65

O God our savior, you are the hope of all the ends of the earth
and of those far off across the sea—
you are robed in power;
you set up the mountains by your might.
You silence the roaring of the seas,
the roaring of their waves,
the tumult of the peoples.
Distant peoples stand in awe of your marvels;
the places of morning and evening you make shout with joy.

You visit the earth and water it,
making it abundantly fertile.

Your river is filled with water;
you supply people with their grain.
Thus do you prepare it:
you drench its plowed furrows,
and level its ridges.
You soften it with showers,
blessing its young sprouts.
You adorn the year with your bounty;
your paths drip with fruitful rain.
The meadows of the wilderness overflow
and the hills are robed with joy.
The pastures are clothed with flocks,
the valleys blanket themselves with grain;
they cheer and sing together for joy.

I 've just stepped into the little house where I live after a day of hard yard work, tearing up the weeds, removing dried up cow dung, dumping the weeds and dirt down by the creek, and raking up. I'm dirty, sweaty, and exhausted. I moved here a few months ago from New Mexico to a little casita on the edge of a ranch right on the California coast, but we've been working on the abandoned house for months—replacing doors, putting in new appliances, fixing the plumbing, and painting it. Spring has arrived and it's time to clear out the walls of weeds around the house. I'm making slow but steady progress. I find it invigorating, but it is tiring. And yet I'm determined to spend time outdoors every day—working on the little yard, walking by the ocean, hiking the coastline trails.

If I find yard work hard, imagine the work of God tending to Mother Earth! You, God, are the one doing all the work for creation, Psalm 65 announces. You have been creating and tending to Mother Earth since the beginning of time, and you have never stopped. You are still working away, taking care of the mountains and hills, the oceans and seas, the trees and fields, the streams and meadows, not to mention the creatures and humans.

Scripture teaches that we are called to tend to creation too, to be good stewards of Mother Earth. Alas, we have failed miserably, and catastrophic climate change is upon us. In the face of this global nightmare, we have to change our lives, stop digging up fossil fuels, use only renewable energy, and dig in to help Mother Earth survive in peace. She doesn't need us to survive, but we need her, and if humanity is to survive, we had all pitch in and help out. That means building the global grassroots movement of nonviolence to end all injustice and wars, fund alternative sources of energy, clean up the earth, and do everything we can to fight global warming. One way to stay hopeful, or at least positive, in such a time, is to increase our time outdoors tending to Mother Earth like the Creator does. Every one of us can do that.

The other day I read about a couple who moved twenty years ago onto a big spread of land that had been completely deforested. Over time, they've planted over two million trees, and now the landscape is a lush green valley. A consequence of this dedicated work has been the return of a wide variety of species to the land. Their determination to restore the earth reflects the Creator's ongoing dedication to Mother Earth and our creatures. We do not want to resist the Creator's earth work; we want to assist it and join the campaign!

IV

Taking Refuge in the God of Peace

THE TRUST OF THE PEACEMAKER

In you, God of peace, I take refuge;
let me never be put to shame.
In your justice, deliver me and rescue me.
Be my rock of refuge, my stronghold to save me;
for you are my rock and my fortress.
My God, rescue me from the hand of the wicked,
from the grasp of the violent and those who do evil.
You are my hope, God of peace;
my trust, God of peace, from my youth.

PSALM 71

Keep me safe, O God, in you I take refuge;
you are my only good.
I keep the God of peace always before me.
With the God of peace at my right
I shall never be shaken.
Therefore my heart is glad, my soul rejoices.

PSALM 16

✻

All who take refuge in you will be glad
and forever shout with joy.

PSALM 5

✻

Blessed are those who find refuge in you,
whose hearts are set on pilgrim roads.
As they pass through the valley of Baca,
they will find spring water to drink.

PSALM 84

15 **Our One True Refuge**
PSALMS 2, 5

Blessed are all who take refuge in the God of peace.

The Buddhists have an ancient teaching that encourages practitioners to "take refuge" in the dharma. In other words, day or night, when all goes well, and when all else fails, turn back to the Buddha's teachings and rest in them and their practice. Return to your breath, enter the present moment, breathe in peace, meditate in stillness, live mindfully, and offer unconditional compassion to yourself and all sentient beings. If you do this morning, noon, and night, you will be safe and sound and at peace, come what may.

The psalms speak of God in the same way. God is our one true refuge indeed, available at any hour of the day. When all is lost, when all goes well, morning, noon, or night, we can turn to the God of peace, take a deep breath, enter into God's peaceful presence, offer a prayer for help, and find true rest in the God who loves us personally and unconditionally.

In that moment, we find refuge in God, and all is transformed; all becomes well; all is peace. If we make the God of peace our daily living refuge, and return to God throughout our day, over and over again, then we will have a strong foundation of peace and security throughout our lives that no calamity, crisis, sickness, or death can take from us. We will live and die in the peace of God because we have spent our days taking refuge in the God of peace.

In this way, the God of peace becomes our one true home. We are at home with God. We know where we belong. We feel safe with God and discover that, indeed, we are safe with the God of peace. This practice becomes a lived experience. We actually feel safe, at peace, at home, in our refuge, in our meditation practice with the God of peace.

So the psalms beg the question: where do we take refuge? If we are honest, we notice that we take refuge anywhere but in God. We find comfort in television, bad news, food, alcohol, drugs, sex, money, possessions, guns, power, and our own egos. We get addicted and, over time, find ourselves stuck in a rut. We think such things will help us, protect us, keep us safe, even provide a haven for us, but none of them help. Most of them take control over our lives and make us feel even more insecure, more fearful, more unsafe, more anxious. As we expand this unwise habit, we realize that collectively we take refuge in nationalism, patriotism, the government, the military, our politicians, our police, our corporations, our entertainment—in anyone or anything but God. As we place our refuge in everything but the God of peace, we succumb to the culture's mindlessness, violence, and injustice. If we claim faith in God, it's a false god named by the culture who hates the same people we hate, a god of violence who blesses our wars, a god of war who promises to help us kill our enemies.

No sane, thoughtful person takes refuge in violence. As we reflect on that truth, we realize that we need to try to take refugee more and more in peace, and that means within the boundaries of nonviolence. Wisdom invites us to take refuge in the living God of peace and nonviolence and find a security and depth that the culture of violence and war cannot offer.

This predicament touches us all. The psalms encourage us to break free from our insecurities and the violence of the culture and turn back to the God of peace and discover there a true safe haven of peace where we can dwell for the rest of our lives. This is the basic journey of the spiritual life—awakening from the mindless culture of violence and war, embarking on a journey to the God of peace, and learning how to live in that refuge through the daily practice and witness of loving nonviolence.

We don't turn to the God of peace because we have been brainwashed by the culture of violence, and the cultural church, to believe in a false god of hatred, violence, and war. This false god, who is often presented as the true God, is mean, violent, ruthless, dangerous, hateful, and threatening. We have created this false god in our own violent image, so we know well what we are talking about when we describe god as blessing our troops, condemning other people to hell, urging us to hate people we don't approve, and encouraging us to make as much money as we can for ourselves.

Jesus shattered all those false images of God. He announced to the scandal of everyone that the one, true, living God is the God of unconditional love, boundless compassion, infinite mercy, total nonviolence, and deep eternal peace. These concepts, words, and images sail over our heads because we have no idea what he is talking about. We understand violence and hatred; we do not understand nonviolence and universal love, much less a God of nonviolence and universal love. We have never seen or experienced such wonders.

In Psalm 5, we hear the beginning descriptions of this God of peace and love:

> *You are not a god who delights in evil;*
> *no wicked person finds refuge with you. The boastful cannot stand*
> *before your eyes.*
> *You hate all who do evil.*
> *You destroy all who speak lies. You abhor murderers and deceivers.*
> *But I can enter your house because of your great love.*
> *I can worship in your holy temple because of my reverence*
> *for you.*

Guide me in your justice because of my enemies.
    Make straight your way before me.
Then let all who take refuge in you be glad and forever shout
        for joy.
Protect them that you may be the joy of those who love
        your name.
For you bless the just. You cover them with favor like a shield.

Jesus invites us to seek and worship the living God of universal love and peace, who is not like us but who created us to be just like him. He announced that this God is infinitely loving, gentle, nonviolent, and peaceful and that we could trust this God, serve this God, follow this God, welcome this God into our hearts, and make our homes with this God. The implication is that we would discover how good it is to dwell in the presence of unconditional love, boundless compassion, total nonviolence, and infinite mercy.

We need not rely on the unhappy culture of violence, greed, or war anymore. We need not trust in our weapons, our money, our government, our military, or our false leaders. With the instructions of the nonviolent Jesus, fulfilling all the teachings of the psalms, we can know the God of peace, learn to share the peace of God with all humanity, and spend our lives on a journey to the God of peace. This is a life worth pursuing.

~~~

The invitation to take refuge in God, to place our trust in God, and to find our security in God, and not in the false gods of the culture, runs throughout the psalms.

> *Lord my God, in you I take refuge; save me … .*
> *God is my shield, who saves the honest heart.* PSALM 7

I take refuge in the God of peace….
The Lord tests the good and the bad, and hates those who love
    violence…
You, God of peace, are just and you love righteous deeds; the upright
    shall see your face. PSALM 11

The poor have the Lord as their refuge. PSALM 14

Keep me safe, O God; in you I take refuge.
I say to the God of peace, you are my Lord, you are my only good.
I keep you always before me;
with you at my right, I shall never be shaken.
Therefore my heart is glad, my soul rejoices; my body also dwells
    secure.
You will show me the path to life,
abounding joy in your presence, the delights at your right hand
    forever. PSALM 16

I love you, Lord my strength,
you are my rock, my fortress, my deliverer,
my God, my rock of refuge, my shield, my saving horn, my
    stronghold. PSALM 18

In you, God of peace, I take refuge; do not let me ever
    be put to shame.
In your justice deliver me; incline your ear to me.
Rescue me quickly!
Be my rock of refuge, a stronghold to save me.
You are my rock and my fortress;
for your name's sake lead and guide me…
into your hands I commit my spirit.

You will redeem me, faithful God….
I will rejoice and be glad in your love….
How abundant is your goodness, God of peace, stored up for those
    who fear you….
You hide them in the shelter of your presence….
You keep them in your abode, safe from plotting tongues.
Blessed be the God of peace who has shown me wondrous love.
Love the God of peace, all you faithful.
The Lord protects the loyal.
Be strong and take heart, all you who hope in the God of peace.
PSALM 31

Even if all hell is breaking loose around us, God will protect those who take refuge in God. Here, for example, is Psalm 3:

God of peace, you are a shield around me; my glory, you keep my
    head high.
Whenever I cried out to the Lord, I was answered from the holy
    mountain.
Whenever I lay down and slept, the Lord sustained me to rise again.
I am not afraid of ten thousand people arrayed against me on every
    side.
Safety comes from the God of peace.

In Psalm 4, we hear the same:

Answer me when I call, my saving God.
In my troubles, you cleared a way; show me favor, hear my prayer….
You have given my heart more joy than they have when grain and
    wine abound.

I shall lie down and sleep in peace, for you alone, God of peace, make me secure.

If we take refuge in God, and call upon God for help, and trust in God, God will protect us, answer our call, be with us, and give us peace. Later, the psalms will also teach the opposite: if you do not place your trust in God, God will not be there to protect you. If you place your security in something else, such as a sword, a weapon, a gun, a nuclear bomb, or a bank account, then that is where your security will be, and you will lose faith in God and trust only in your weapons and money. One day, when they fail you, because they cannot protect you, you will look for God, but you will have turned away from God long ago. Instead of waiting for that moment, the psalms urge us to build a life based on faithful trust in God.

If we have swords, guns, weapons, and money, we do not need God. Our security and safety are found in our weapons. But if we have no weapons, if we are nonviolent, we need God. We have no one else to protect us. Our lives are completely rooted in faith and truth in this nonviolent God who sides with the nonviolent.

The lesson: if we dare take refuge in the God of peace and nonviolence, we have to get rid of our guns, quit the military, non-cooperate with the culture of violence, and enter the boundaries of nonviolence for the rest of our lives. We have to be as nonviolent as Jesus; we need to place all our trust and hope in the God of peace and find our safety, security, and sanity there. This is what we do every day when we sit quietly in the peace of God, and rest in God, and abide in God. We try to make our home in the God of peace, and so from now on, as we take refuge in God, we live in the peace of God, and we become instruments of God's disarming love for others.

16 God Alone, God Alone, God Alone
PSALM 62

My soul rests in God alone,
from whom comes my salvation.
God alone is my rock and salvation,
my fortress; I shall never fall.....

My soul, be at rest in God alone,
from whom comes my hope.
God alone is my rock and my salvation,
my fortress; I shall not fall.
My safety and honor are with God,
my strong rock; my refuge is with God.
Trust God at all times, O people!
Pour out your hearts to God our refuge!

What attracted Thomas Merton most to the Abbey of Gethsemani when he first arrived there in Bardstown, Kentucky, Holy Week 1941, was the stark message "God alone" over the entranceway. Think about that. Who would want God alone? Apparently, that was exactly what Merton was looking for, even though he didn't realize it until that moment. He had tried everything the world had to offer, from travel to alcohol and sex to communism and jazz to literature and laughter, and found that nothing worked. Everything left him empty. He was worse than ever.

Then he discovered God. He started to pray, went to Mass, became a Catholic, and decided to give his life to God. When he entered the Abbey, he began prayer as a way of life. He spent seven hours in communal prayer every day for the next twenty-seven years. He tried to live in permanent conscious communion with God—and more, open to all the social, economic, and political implications of life in union with the God of peace and love.

For Trappists, the psalms were the essential form of prayer. They chanted them morning, noon, and night. They read through the psalms nearly every week. That meant, for Merton and the monks, trying to live the teaching of Psalm 62 every minute every day: "My soul rests in God alone."

Merton was a towering intellectual. Over the years he studied every aspect of the spiritual life, including the ancient Hindu sages who would whisper the name "God" over and over all day long for years on end. These holy ones spent their entire lives calling upon God. They literally talked themselves into holiness, sanctity, peace, and eternity. Gandhi practiced this, too, along with his friend, the famous yogi, Paramahansa Yogananda, author of *Autobiography of a Yogi*.

Psalm 62 invites us to focus on God morning, noon, and night, to live first and foremost for God from now on, for the rest of our lives unto death, that is, to love God with all our heart, all our soul, all our mind, and all our strength, as the gospel instructs. We do not have to be Trappist monks or Hindu yogis, but we can call upon the name of God morning, noon, and night and live full-time for God. This is doable, if we commit ourselves to it.

My soul rests in God alone. Trust God at all times. This is what we do as we take time each day for meditation, as we read the Scriptures and the lives of the saints, as we receive the sacraments, and as we return to God throughout our days. We place our hope in God. We trust in God. We let God be our refuge, safety, sanctuary, rock, strength, and stronghold and discover in the process the blessings of safety and glory, hope and peace, power and loving-kindness. We discover that it feels good to rest in God alone, to trust in God, to leave the outcome in God's hands. No one told us this, but as we try it, we feel an immense sense of relief. Nothing else has worked, as Merton discovered. But this works.

It is a matter of quiet meditation every day, turning to God, looking to God, hoping in God, listening to God, resting in God, adoring God, and finding God everywhere. We arrange our lives so that, interiorly, we are naturally focused on God all the time, as a matter of course, as our ordinary, daily, normal way of life, whether anyone else knows or not. In fact, it's better if no one else knows this, our inner secret, our secret relationship with the God of peace.

We believe in God, come what may, no matter what, in good times and bad. We place our hope in God, find our security in God, renounce all pretenders to the throne (money, America, patriotism, the military, guns, the NRA, power, possessions, pride—whatever), and take refuge in God and so surrender completely to God. This becomes our quiet, innermost, personal reality, our permanent search for and reliance on God. It is one way to describe the spiritual life, to describe our very lives. But the psalm continues:

> *Mortals are a mere breath,*
> *the powerful but an illusion;*
> *in the balances they go up;*
> *together they are lighter than air.*
> *Do not trust in extortion;*
> *and put no empty hopes in robbery.*
> *Though wealth increase,*
> *do not set your heart upon it.*
>
> *One thing God has said,*
> *two things I have heard:*
> *power belongs to God;*
> *and so does steadfast kindness and mercy.*
> *For you repay each of us*
> *according to our deeds.*

Here is a helpful teaching. Right there, in black and white, the psalmist insists: don't trust in the powerful; don't believe them. They seem powerful, but they are lighter than air, an empty hope. Don't trust them or extortion or robbery or even money at all. Trust only God.

With God there is true power, true kindness, true mercy—the only things that matter. The choice we make regarding these matters have eternal consequences. We are advised to live life according to the right choice and let the consequences of our Godly trust lead us one day into God.

17 Put No Trust in Princes or Presidents, Only the God of Peace
PSALM 146

Psalm 146 urges us to place our trust and hope in God, but it teaches at the start that we cannot do that if, at the same time, we are placing our trust and hope in "princes," that is, in any ruler. It's one or the other—the God of peace and justice, or the rulers of this world.

This is a hard teaching for anyone to accept, but it's critical to the life of faith. Where do we place our trust? In the God of peace, or in President Obama? President Trump? President Bush? The believer does not place their attention, their intentions, their soul in any leader. We know how corrupt and violent they are, no matter how seemingly liberal or conservative. God alone deserves our political allegiance. When we give one hundred percent of our souls to the God of peace, then we pray with the psalmist:

> Praise the God of peace, my soul;
> I will praise the God of peace all my life,
> I will praise God my whole life long.

Put no trust in princes,
in mortals, powerless to save.
When they breathe their last, they return to the earth;
that day, all their plans perish.

A key reason not to trust in rulers and only in God is because only God can bring real justice, liberation, and healing. No prince, president, or dictator will ever do that. Here the psalm begins to unpack the politics of God. In this time of division, hatred, and war, it is worth taking time to hear the psalmist's declaration about God's politics and then to ask ourselves if we want to be on the side of God's politics or some other false ruler:

Happy are those whose help is the God of peace,
whose hope is in the God of peace,
the maker of heaven and earth,
the seas and all that is in them,
who keeps faith forever,
secures justice for the oppressed,
who gives bread to the hungry,
who sets prisoners free,
who opens the eyes of the blind,
who lifts up those who are bowed down,
who loves the righteous,
who protects the immigrant,
who comes to help the orphan and the widow,
but thwarts the way of the wicked.
The God of peace shall reign forever.

This list of God's political attributes is stunning and hopeful: God keeps faith forever; brings justice for the oppressed; gives bread to the hungry; sets prisoners free; gives sight to the blind; raises up those pushed down; loves the righteous; protects the immigrant; comes to the aid of the orphan and the widow (the victims of war); and thwarts the way of the wicked, those in power. Then the punch line: God's reign of peace shall last forever!

Here the psalm outlines a politics of peace, a politics of justice, and a politics of nonviolence greater than any of us can imagine. These days, we are stuck in a politics of war, injustice, and violence, which engages in the exact opposite of God's good works. The politics of the world, beginning with the politics of the United States, are the politics of death. The world's politics do not keep faith; do not bring justice but injustice; do not give bread to the hungry but let the hungry starve; do not set prisoners free but rather puts them away for life, executes them, and builds more prisons; do not give sight to the blind but keep people in the dark; do not raise up those pushed down but push people even further down into total helplessness; do not love the righteous but the hypocrites; do not protect the immigrant but hunt them, arrest them, jail them, and kill them; do not help the victims of war but try to kill them too; and most of all, they reward the wicked for their wickedness. This is our predicament today.

But the world, the US government, Fox News, and the *New York Times* will never tell us that all this is fading, that only God's reign of peace will last, and that God's reign of peace, not America's empire of war, is worth pursuing.

Jesus picked up on these teachings and spent his life practicing these politics of justice and nonviolence and calling us to enter God's reign of peace. This, the psalmist teaches, is what life is about. We too can choose to practice God's politics, to welcome God's reign of peace in our hearts and lives, and to spend our days praising the God of peace. Like Jesus, we can put our full trust in God and enter eternal life now by living in God's reign and practicing God's politics. Why not pursue such a lofty spiritual goal? Life is too short to waste our time doing anything else.

18 You Are My Strong Refuge; I Will Speak of Your Mighty Works
PSALM 71

I was raised Catholic in a remote North Carolina town and educated by wonderful, young, kind nuns. I was interested in the church from day one, mainly because Jesus seemed to be such a likeable and good person. I thought about God, and then I started noticing the presence of God around me.

I distinctly remember one morning, for example, when I was about four or five years old, getting up around 6 AM on a Saturday, going outside into the summer air, sitting on our swing set as the sun rose, and being overwhelmed by the loving, peaceful presence of God. After such consolations, I tried to seek God on a daily basis. I've been trying ever since. I want to be with God, rely on God, and take refuge in God. These days, now that I am old and gray, I'm still trying, still seeking, and still searching.

That's the hope and prayer of Psalm 71. I've been hoping in you all my life, from my youth until now, the psalmist says. You have always been my refuge, my rock, my fortress. Continue to be so, and even now, I will praise you and proclaim your name to the vast assembly. This is the prayer of each one of us; each one of us has been hoping and seeking God all our lives.

> In you, God of peace, I take refuge;
> let me never be put to shame.
> In your justice, deliver me and rescue me.
> Be my rock of refuge, my stronghold to save me;

for you are my rock and my fortress.
My God, rescue me from the hand of the wicked,
from the grasp of the violent and those who do evil.
You are my hope, God of peace;
my trust, God of peace, from my youth.
On you I have depended since birth;
from my mother's womb you are my strength;
my hope in you never wavers.

I have become a portent to many,
but you are my strong refuge!
My mouth is filled with your praise,
I shall sing of your glory every day.

Do not cast me off in my old age;
do not forsake me when my strength fails.
For my enemies speak against me;
they watch and plot against me.
They say, "God has abandoned that person.
Pursue and seize the one whom God has forsaken!… "
But I will always hope in you
and praise you more and more.
My mouth shall proclaim your just deeds,
day after day your acts of deliverance,
though I cannot number them all.
I will speak of the mighty works of the God of peace;
I will tell of your justice.

God, from my youth you have taught me;
to this day I proclaim your wondrous deeds.
do not forsake me, God,

now that I am old and gray,
that I may proclaim your might
to all generations yet to come.
Your power and your justice, God,
reach to the highest heaven.
You have done great things;
O God, who is your equal?

Psalm 71 announces that God has been faithful to us, throughout our clumsy lifelong spiritual search and journey. Because of God's fidelity, kindness, and good deeds, we will not only try to be faithful but proclaim what God has done far and wide.

This, too, is an important teaching. When I was in my early twenties, my friend Daniel Berrigan taught me that it's not so much that we are political but that we are public. We go public with our faith and peacemaking, he said. We talk about it, proclaim it, write about it, and engage people everywhere with the good news of the God of peace, the way of disarmament and nonviolence, and the hope of nonviolent transformation. We don't have to be superstars like Bono or George Harrison, but we can gently proclaim our hope and trust in the God of peace and help others place their hope and trust in God too. As we do this, we place our focus not on ourselves but on others. As we continue to live in God, we spend our remaining years serving humanity, pointing to the God of peace, and trying to help God's global peace movement of nonviolent transformation for Mother Earth and creation. We speak of the mighty works of the God of peace, not the violent works of the nations and their rulers. In this way, we show others that we have indeed lived our lives in the refuge of the God of peace.

V

Give Us Peace, God of Peace

THE CRY OF THE PEACEMAKER

Blessed are those whose help is Jacob's God,
who put their hope in the God of peace,
who made heaven and earth,
the sea, and all that is in them,
who keeps faith forever,
secures justice for the oppressed,
and gives food to the hungry.
The God of peace sets prisoners free,
gives sight to the blind,
lifts up those who are bowed down,
loves the righteous,
watches over the strangers,
sustains the orphan and the widow,
but thwarts the way of the wicked.
The God of peace will reign forever.

PSALM 146

19 My God, My God, Why Have You Forsaken Me? ☀ PSALM 22

"My God, my God, why have you forsaken me?"—the last words of the nonviolent Jesus as he dies on the cross, executed by the Roman Empire, a victim of the death penalty. They voice his feeling of total despair, rejection, and abandonment, even and most especially by God. Psalm 22 is a lament of rock-bottom despair. But if you stay with it, you discover that it becomes a hymn of hope. That's what the early gospel readers would have recognized when they heard this line as the dying Jesus' last words. They would have understood his total despair but known that he did not die in that state. Instead, he pushed forward in faith, reclaimed his trust in God, surrendered himself to God in hope, and died consoled and at peace. With this psalm, Jesus discovered true hope, the costly hope that comes with trust in the rock-bottom moment when all hope is lost.

Psalm 22 is the most transformative of psalms, going from one end of the spectrum to another. It starts in the depths of despair and agony and journeys through suffering and rejection, then recalls the good deeds of God and reclaims one's hope in God once again, so that by the end, we trust in God and promise to serve God always.

The first half voices the feelings of utter pain, anguish, rejection, and abandonment and tells the inner turmoil of the crucified, nonviolent Jesus:

> My God, my God, why have you forsaken me?
> Why so far from my call for help, from my cries of anguish?
> O my God, I cry by day, but you do not answer;
> and by night, but I have no rest.
>
> Yet you are enthroned as the Holy One, the glory of Israel.

In you our ancestors trusted; they trusted and you rescued them.
To you they cried and you saved them;
in you they trusted and were not disappointed.

But I am a worm and not human,
scorned by others, despised by the people.
All who see me mock me; they curl their lips and jeer;
they shake their heads at me:
"This one relied on God—so let God deliver;
if God loves this one, God will come to the rescue."

But it was you who drew me from the womb
and made me safe at my mother's breasts.
Upon you I was thrust from the womb;
since my mother bore me, you are my God.

Do not be far from me, for trouble is near,
and there is no one to help.
Many bulls surround me; fierce bulls of Bashan encircle me.
They open their mouths at me, like lions that rend and roar.
Like water my life drains away;
all my bones are out of joint.
My heart has become like wax, melting away within me.
As dry as a potsherd is my throat; my tongue sticks to my palate;
you lay me in the dust of death.
Dogs surround me; a pack of evildoers closes in on me.
They have pierced my hands and my feet;
I can count all my bones.
They stare at me and gloat;
they divide my clothes among them;
for my clothing they cast lots.

This is the voice of one who has been crushed by his enemies, literally crucified and destroyed. Crucifixion was the normal form of capital punishment for revolutionaries, used as a deterrent to stop insurrection. By publicly stripping and executing violent rebels, people would be terrified to join the revolutionary movements to overthrow the empire.

Jesus was totally nonviolent, but he was not passive. He confronted the Roman Empire, regularly broke the law, and led a nonviolent movement to Jerusalem, where he entered the temple and turned over the tables of the money changers in an act of peaceful nonviolent civil disobedience that disrupted business as usual. He didn't hurt anyone or kill anyone; he was meticulously nonviolent; he was a new kind of revolutionary—a nonviolent revolutionary.

His illegal campaign led the ruling authorities to hunt him down and kill him. He was harassed, betrayed, arrested, jailed, tried, tortured, and brutally executed. What the psalm reveals is that while Jesus once felt the presence of the God of peace at every turn, now, at his darkest, lowest moment, he only felt the absence of the God of peace. When Luke puts this psalm on his lips, Jesus becomes the embodiment of all those who once felt loved by God but now feel abandoned by God. This is the journey for all of us, as eventually the bottom falls out of our own lives, whether through illness, accident, the death of a loved one, the loss of home or career, or, most of all, our own impending suffering and eventual death.

To sit with this psalm is to sit before a crucifix and feel the total desolation of Jesus himself. His friends have run away, he has been crushed by the empire, all hope is lost, and he is dying naked on a cross in agony. He remains totally nonviolent until the end, and in his dying breath, this greatest of peacemakers cries out with all the world's poor and oppressed: "My God, my God, why have you forsaken me?" It is at once a cry of all the abandoned, lonely, and hopeless people throughout history, but note—it is still addressed to God. The dying, crucified Jesus still lives in relationship with his beloved God, so he still calls upon God, even though he does not feel the presence of God.

Jesus actually never gives up on God. He just voices his profound disappointment at God's noticeable absence. He had done everything well for God, embodied peace and love, taught the people, healed the sick, proclaimed God's reign, only to be arrested and executed by the Roman Empire. He is completely abandoned by his friends and crushed by the empire, but he feels abandoned by God as well. Yet he transcends his feelings and keeps trusting in God. By calling upon God in this lowest moment in human history, he affirms his faith in God. He cries out for help, for an answer, for relief, and gets no answer, but he still looks to God, and in that process, rekindles his trust in God. This is the paradigmatic journey of faith, hope, and trust in a nutshell. The rest of the psalm voices that spiritual transformation and shows how we too can keep on trusting in God, no matter how abandoned, no matter how crushed:

> But you, God of peace, do not be far away;
> my strength, come quickly to help me.
> Deliver my soul from the sword,
> my life from the power of the dog.
> Save me from the lion's mouth,
> my poor life from the horns of wild bulls.
>
> Then I will proclaim your name to the assembly;
> I will praise you to my brothers and sisters:
> "You who fear God, give praise!
> All descendants of Jacob, give honor;
> show reverence, all descendants of Israel!
> For God has not despised or disdained
> the misery of this wretched one,

God did not turn away from me,
but heard me when I cried out.

I will offer praise in the great assembly;
my vows I will fulfill before those who fear God.
The poor will eat and be satisfied;
those who seek the God of peace will offer praise.
May your hearts enjoy life forever!"

All the ends of the earth will remember and turn to the God of peace;
all the families of nations will worship before God.
For dominion belongs to the God of peace, the ruler over the nations.
All who sleep in the earth will bow low before God;
all who have gone down into the dust will kneel.
I will live for the God of peace; my descendants will serve you.
Future generations will be told of the God of peace,
that they may proclaim to a people yet unborn
all the salvation God has brought.

Deliver me from the sword, from the dog's teeth, the lion's mouth, from the wild bull's horns, from terror, from violence, from death, the rejected one begs. Then, at some point we're told, "God did not turn away from me but heard me when I cried out." Somehow, somewhere in that dark moment, a transformation occurred. The rejected one realized his cry was heard, that he was not actually rejected by God, that in the long haul, God would protect him. He reclaims his faith, hope, and trust in God and promises to tell the whole world about his faithful God. So we read: I will offer praise in the great assembly! I will fulfill my vows before the people! I will live for the God of peace!

With this bold promise to praise God, keep his vows, and live solely for God, the rejected one announces that the poor and hungry will be fed, those who seek the God of peace will praise God, and all people will turn to the God of peace. A remarkable transformation! The psalmist realizes that this pledge to live for the God of peace will bear good fruit. It will bring not only social and economic justice (food for the hungry) but also a global spiritual transformation, as eventually all people will follow and return to the God of peace! This is a cause for rejoicing! Indeed, it is a victory.

As we pray through Psalm 22, and journey from despair to hope, we can ask for the grace to proclaim anew with Jesus on the cross the fidelity of the God of peace and our newfound hope and trust. We too can offer praise for the God of peace in the great assembly. We too can fulfill our vows of peace, love, and nonviolence before all people. We too, from now on, can live for the God of peace. If so, we too will keep our faith, hope, loving trust, and gospel nonviolence alive, come what may, and let our lives someday bear good fruit for peace.

20 **Lead My Soul from Prison**
PSALMS 142, 102, 88

I n December 1993, I was arrested in Goldsboro, North Carolina, with three friends for entering the Seymour Johnson Air Force Base and hammering on an F-15e nuclear capable fighter bomber. We were obeying the word of God: "They shall beat their swords into plowshares and study war no more" (Isaiah 2:4). We were taken in chains to various local jails and then brought down to the Robeson County Jail on the border of South Carolina. It was built for fifty but had over four hundred prisoners, all people of color except us. In the five previous years, twenty-five inmates had died mysteriously, probably at the hands of the guards.

My friends and I were separated, and I was put into a large cell with four bunk beds and a TV on the wall. There I remained for three weeks, before my friends and I were put in a cell together. Those first three weeks were some of the hardest of my life. I was scared and lonely, and the other inmates were mean and violent, so I kept to myself and sat on my top bunk all day long.

Once a fight broke out in front of me. Everyone started yelling at one another, and one inmate stabbed another with a pen, leaving a pool of blood on the floor. He was taken off in a stretcher. On another occasion, three big, mean jailers in uniform and armed with guns called me out into the hallway, holding a box of that day's mail for me—over fifty letters. They yelled at me for getting too much mail and told me to stop it. They had to read all incoming mail in case of contraband. Before I arrived, the jail might receive a total of ten letters each day—for all 400 inmates—and they hated this extra work. I bowed my head, and kept my mouth shut, just hoping they wouldn't beat me up.

I had no visitors, no one to talk to, and no possessions except a Bible. I started to read the psalms and pray through them slowly as best I could. I was surprised to discover how many psalms were set in prison or based on the lamentations of prisoners. Suddenly, I realized they named my rock-bottom despair, depression, and desolation. Sure, I was in jail for a noble cause, trying to do my bit for nuclear disarmament, but I felt rejected by many people for my public witness. The psalms helped me to cry out to God and beg for help.

It's hard to describe being in jail. It's like being locked in an ugly, dirty bathroom at some remote, awful gas station and being kept there for a year. I wrote letters and articles but found I could not pray. I've been told that when you are sick and dying in a hospital, you can't pray either, so I always compared prison to being in a hospital.

I had just been ordained a priest and had prepared for many years for this action. I had spoken out and written about disarmament, aspired to Gandhi's and King's lives of civil disobedience and nonviolent resistance, and practiced daily meditation. Now that I found myself behind bars; my world caved in and I crashed. Many people were scandalized by my action and told me so in no uncertain terms. I lost a lot of friends. I also felt the palpable absence of God, which was new and unexpected, because for years, I had felt the consoling presence of God. I cried out with the psalms and wallowed in despair.

~~~

Over two million people sit in prison today in the United States, some on death row, waiting to be executed. Millions more suffer in abominable jails around the world. The Scriptures make clear that God is on the side of prisoners, and in Jesus, God became a prisoner. To pray the psalms is to pray in solidarity with prisoners everywhere and to explore the depths of our own inner despair and desolation, to offer it to the God of peace, and to beg for the grace of peace, love, and consolation. Psalm 142 offers a typical prisoner's prayer:

> *With my voice I cry to the God of peace;*
> *with my voice I beseech the God of peace.*
> *Before God I pour out my complaint;*
> *I tell God all my troubles.*
> *When my spirit is faint within me, you know my path.*
> *Along the path I walk, they have hidden a trap for me.*
> *I look to my right hand to see*
> *that there is no one willing to notice me.*
> *There is no escape for me; no one cares for me.*
>
> *I cry out to you, God of peace.*
> *I say, "You are my refuge, my portion in the land of the living.*
> *Listen to my cry for help, for I am brought very low.*
> *Rescue me from my persecutors, for they are too strong for me.*

Lead me out of prison,
so that I may give thanks to your name.
Then the righteous shall gather around me,
for you have been very good to me."

~~~

I faced twenty years in prison, was convicted in court of several felony charges, served nine months in tiny country jails cells, but then was released and put under house arrest for two more years. I didn't know that I was going to be released so soon and expected to do at least five years in prison. Eventually, my friends and I landed in the Edenton County Jail, which could hold thirty men. Because there was so much publicity about us, the warden, who grew fond of us, was worried: in order to protect us, he put us in isolation. That meant we were locked in a tiny cell and basically never left it for the next eight months. The food came through a slot in the door. We had bunk beds, a toilet, and a TV. That's it. It took us six weeks to get a Bible. Thank God, the mail still poured in every day.

After about five months of being locked in that tiny room my life seemed to come to a complete standstill, and the walls began to close in on me. My friends and I developed a strict monastic schedule. The discipline would help us survive and find a modicum of peace and purpose. I still found it extremely difficult to meditate. Instead, we became involuntary Buddhas, just sitting still, breathing in and out, depressed but totally mindful, lonely but centered, feeling God's absence yet filled with grace. Each day lasted one year. One day at a time did not work for me, nor did one hour at a time. I remember months of living "one minute at a time," just trying to get through the next minute in peace. My spirit was crushed; half of it was gone. (You can feel some of this in the journal I published from those difficult days, *Peace Behind Bars.*)

Psalm 102 offers the prayer I would have said if I could have. It voices the pain of those who have hit rock bottom, starting with prisoners:

God of peace, hear my prayer; let my cry come to you.
Do not hide your face from me in the day of my distress.
Turn your ear to me; answer me right away when I call.
For my days pass away like smoke;
my bones burn as in a furnace.
My heart is withered, dried up like grass;
I am too wasted to eat my food.
From my loud groaning I become just skin and bones.
I am like a desert owl, like a little owl among the ruins.
I lie awake and moan; I am like a lone sparrow on the roof.
All day long my enemies taunt me;
in their rage, they use my name for a curse.
I eat ashes like bread, mingle my drink with tears.
Because of your anger, you lifted me up just to throw me down.
My days are like a lengthening shadow; I wither away
    like the grass.

But you, God of peace, are enthroned forever;
your renown lasts for all generations.
You will again show mercy to Zion;
now is the time for pity; the appointed time has come....
The nations shall honor your name, God of peace,
and all the kings of the earth, your glory.
For you, God of peace, will rebuild Zion;
you will appear in your glory.
You will heed the plea of the lowly, not scorning their prayer.
Let this be written for the next generation,
for a people not yet born, that they may praise the God of peace;

"The God of peace looked down from the holy heights
and viewed the earth from heaven.
The God of peace heard the groaning of the prisoners,
and set free those doomed to die."
Then, God of peace, your name will be declared on Zion, your praise
      in Jerusalem,
when peoples and kingdoms gather to serve the God of peace.
God has shattered my strength in mid-course, has cut short my days.
O my God, I plead, do not take me in the midst of my days.
Your years last through all generations.
Of old you laid the earth's foundations;
the heavens are the work of your hands.
They perish, but you endure;
they all wear out like a garment;
like clothing you change them and they are changed.
But you are the same; your years have no end.
May the children of your servants live on;
may their descendants live in your presence.

My days had ended. There were no more days. I was locked in a cell.
I could groan, but really, I couldn't even do that. Instead, it was like
deep-sea diving, like I was living in slow motion, walking on the moon,
entering another time zone, living in some kind of "twilight zone."

I was never physically hurt, but I was yelled at, handcuffed period-
ically, mocked, and humiliated all day long for months. My heart defi-
nitely withered; yes, I was like a nighttime owl in the desert, all alone,
calling out. But I knew too, in faith, that the God of peace knew exactly
where my friends and I were, what we had done, and what we were enduring; I knew that God kept watch over us. This kind of trust was very
deep, a trust beyond words, and that's why I could feel the rest of the
psalm too. I knew one day the God of peace would be praised, honored,

and obeyed, and perhaps we were doing our little part to herald that coming day. We knew God would attend to us prisoners, we believed that one day humanity would serve the God of peace, and so we struggled one minute at a time, like the psalmist, to keep hope alive.

～

The story of the gospel is the story of God taking sides with the poor, the oppressed, the imprisoned, the lonely, the abandoned, the immigrant, and the enemy. God has come to liberate us all through the power of active nonviolence and universal love. As disciples of the nonviolent Jesus, we too are invited to take sides with the poor, the oppressed, the imprisoned, the lonely, the abandoned, the immigrant, and the enemy. From now on, we live in universal solidarity with the poorest of the poor, with "the least of these," as Christ does.

And so, when we read and pray through these psalms of lamentation, we pray with the poor, the oppressed, the imprisoned, and the wounded people of the world, and we beg God for our liberation, for a new day of freedom, justice, and nonviolence for all.

With Psalm 88, we stand with the least and cry out with them; we beg the God of peace for an end to injustice, oppression, imprisonment, violence, and war, for the coming of God's reign of peace, justice, and nonviolence, here and now. As we pray this psalm, we pray with all the saints, martyrs, and prophets of history who stood for justice and peace, only to be humiliated, rejected, mocked, arrested, imprisoned, and killed. With them, with Jesus on the cross, we turn to God, surrender ourselves to God, and try to place our hope and the hope of all the world's poor in God.

> *God of my salvation,*
> *at night, I cry aloud in your presence.*
> *Let my prayer come before you;*

incline your ear to my cry.
For my soul is filled with troubles;
my life draws near to Sheol.
I am counted among those who go down to the pit;
I am like a warrior without strength.
My couch is among the dead,
like the slain who lie in the grave,
whom you remember no more;
they are cut off from you.
You plunge me into the bottom of the pit,
into the deep and dark abyss.
Your wrath lies heavy upon me;
all your waves crash over me.
Because of you my companions shun me;
you make me loathsome to them;
caged in, I cannot escape;
my eyes grow dim from trouble and sorrow.
Every day I call on you, God of peace;
I stretch out my hands to you.
Do you work wonders for the dead?
Do the shades rise up and praise you?
Is your mercy proclaimed in the grave,
your faithful love among those who have perished?
Are your marvels known in the darkness,
your saving help in the land of oblivion?

But I cry out to you, God of peace;
in the morning my prayer comes before you.
Why do you reject me, God of peace?
Why hide your face from me?
I have been mortally afflicted since youth;

I have borne your terrors and I am made numb.
Your wrath has swept over me;
your assaults have destroyed me.
All day they surround me like a flood;
from every side they encircle me.
Because of you, friend and neighbor shun me;
my only friend is darkness.

21 I Clothed Myself in Sackcloth, It Is on Your Account I Bear Insult
PSALMS 69, 30

Psalm 69 cries out in pain to God over injustice, rejection, and persecution. It sounds like the writer has been falsely charged with stealing and is hated by everyone. The psalmist is crushed and angry but, in the end, turns to God and hopes in God still.

I suggest we read this lament from the perspective of the nonviolent Jesus and let it take on an entirely deeper emotional story. Jesus came among us, gentle and peaceful, and taught us the way of peace, love, and nonviolence. He healed the sick, forgave everyone, fed people, and built a community of peace. Then he launched an anti-empire campaign of nonviolence to confront injustice. He walked all the way from the outback to Jerusalem, where he engaged in dangerous public, nonviolent civil disobedience in the temple. He denounced the Roman Empire and invited everyone to turn instead to God's reign of peace and nonviolence. Within forty-eight hours, he was betrayed, arrested, abandoned, denied, jailed, tried, mocked, tortured, and executed. He died on the cross dejected, crushed, and alone but hoping in God unto his last breath.

This is the person we claim to follow, and you have to admit he must want us to confront systemic injustice, war, and imperial domination.

His way is not a way of passive indifference. He does not sit all day under a tree and teach us to do likewise. He does not avoid controversy or want us to avoid controversy. Everything about him is controversial. He wants us to take on the world head on—but do it nonviolently.

For Jesus, the way to God is to disrupt our unjust society, to rock the boat for the sake of justice, to shake things up so that people wake up and reject empire. He agitates for justice and peace and pays a great price for it. In a culture of violence and war, this never goes over well. People respond to public prophetic work for justice and peace by denouncing us, mocking us, harassing us, even arresting and jailing us. Nonetheless, I submit, this is the Christian journey—to follow the nonviolent Jesus by resisting and confronting empire and the culture of violence with the full force of active nonviolence and to accept the consequences of our public peacemaking with grace and nonviolence.

If you have ever stood up against racism, war, nuclear weapons, environmental destruction, or governmental injustice, you know what it is to be mocked and rejected. You understand the gospel and Psalm 69. If you have not, you don't know what they're talking about. But it's never too late to take a public stand, speak out, sit in, and agitate for justice, disarmament, and creation.

Psalm 69 can be read from the perspective of all those who follow the nonviolent Jesus on the path of public confrontation against war and injustice, those who rocked the ship of state and paid the consequences. From that Jesus perspective, it reminds us to call on God, accept the consequences, and hope in the power of our nonviolence to sow seeds of social transformation. It tells us we are fulfilling our job description—paying the price for peace.

~~~

As I read this psalm, I think of my twenty years leading a public campaign against the US nuclear weapons laboratories in Los Alamos,

New Mexico. When I first arrived in New Mexico as a parish priest out in the boondocks, I started an annual vigil every August on Hiroshima Day to call for nuclear disarmament. Within a few years, hundreds of people were joining us, and we received statewide press coverage. That led to public rejection and denunciations from people across the state, beginning with the church and my parishioners. We faced counter protests, hate mail, editorials against us, and I myself received a few threats. The hardest rejection for me was the mean response of the cold Catholic archbishop, who called me into his office and forbade me to pray publicly for peace. "Nuclear weapons are our only security," he said. "God can't protect us from rogue states," he added. A year or two later, he removed my priestly faculties granting me permission to say Mass, and I had to leave the state. I was treated far worse the pedophile priests—all because I was against war—that is, I was against the killing of children. Like most other Christians, he thought that was permissible. I know I have already written about this, but I'm still stymied by the whole experience!

For the sixtieth anniversary of Hiroshima, we turned to the Book of Jonah and decided to try out the symbolic nonviolent action of the people of Nineveh. We made three hundred pieces of sackcloth and three hundred bags of ashes, gathered people in the park where the original Hiroshima bomb was built, marched through Los Alamos toward the labs, and at the appointed time, poured ashes on the ground, put on our sackcloth, and sat down for thirty minutes of silent prayer and public repentance for the mortal sin of war and nuclear weapons. We've been doing this every year since.

I identify with the psalmist, who says I've fasted, prayed, even clothed myself in sackcloth—all for your cause—only to face harassment, rejection, and abuse. Like the psalmist, I too looked for compassion—especially among church people, even the church leadership—and found none.

For those who have undergone the difficult consequences of public peace work in a culture of war, Psalm 69 gives voice to the pain we have undergone and encourages us to carry on and hope still in God. So we pray with the psalmist:

Save me, O God, for the waters have reached my neck.
I have sunk into the deep mire, where there is no foothold.
I have gone down into deep waters;
the flood overwhelms me.
I am weary with crying out; my throat is dry.
My eyes fail from looking for my God.
More numerous than the hairs of my head
are those who hate me without cause.
Those who would destroy me are mighty,
but they accuse me falsely.
Must I now restore what I did not steal?

God, you know my folly; my faults are not hidden from you.
Let those who wait in hope for you, God of peace, not be shamed
  because of me.
Let those who seek you, God of Israel, not be disgraced because of me.
It is for your sake that I bear insult, that disgrace covers my face.
I have become an outcast to my family, a stranger
  to my mother's children.
Because zeal for your house has consumed me,
I am scorned by those who scorn you.
They insulted me when I humbled my soul with fasting.
When I clothed myself in sackcloth, I became a byword for them.
Those who sit in the gate gossip about me;
drunkards make up songs about me.

But I will pray to you, God of peace.
In your abundant kindness, answer me.
Rescue me and do not let me sink into the mire.
Save me from those who hate me
and from the watery depths.
Do not let the flood overwhelm me,
or the deep swallow me up, or the pit close its mouth over me.
Answer me, God of peace, in your generous love;
turn to me in your great mercy.
Do not hide your face from your servant;
come quickly to answer me, for I am in distress.
Come and redeem my life;
set me free from my enemies.
You know the insults I endure, my shame, my disgrace;
you know all my foes.
Insult has broken my heart, and I am in despair;
I looked for compassion, but there was none, for comforters,
*   but found none.*
Instead they gave me poison for food;
and vinegar for my thirst ... .

I am miserable and in pain; let your saving help protect me, God,
that I may praise your name in song and glorify you
*   with thanksgiving.*
That will please the God of peace more than oxen,
or a bull with horns and hooves:
"See, you lowly ones, and be glad;
you who seek God, let your hearts rise!
For the God of peace hears the poor,
and does not despise those in bondage.
Let the heaven and the earth praise our Creator,
the seas and everything in them!

For God will rescue Zion, and rebuild the cities of Judah.
God's people will live there and possess it;
the descendants of God's servants will inherit it;
those who love God's name will dwell in it.

∾

Addendum: When I read Psalm 69, I think of Psalm 30 as the antidote. In Psalm 69, the writer cries out to God to be saved from those who mock him, even as the writer fasts and sits in sackcloth. Psalm 30 announces that God has turned the psalmist's mourning into gladness. The writer no longer has to wear sackcloth but has been clothed with gladness.

I like to imagine what this would be like—one day, never again to have to put on sackcloth and sit in ashes like an utter fool outside a building where they build weapons of mass destruction that can blow up the planet twenty times over. As long as there are nuclear weapons, we need to fast, repent, and sit in sackcloth and ashes. Only on the day when all nuclear weapons are outlawed and abolished will we be clothed in gladness.

The psalm holds out the promise that that great day is possible—and coming! That will be another Easter day for humanity, when death has been overcome, when loving nonviolence has transformed the culture of violence, when peace has disarmed our warring hearts. On that day, we will praise the God of peace, with Psalm 30:

> *I praise you, God of peace, for you raised me up*
> *and did not let my foes rejoice over me.*
> *God of peace, I cried out to you for help and you healed me.*
> *You brought my soul up from Sheol; you pulled me from the pit*
> *and let me live.*

Sing praises to the God of peace, you faithful; give thanks
        to God's holy memory.
For God's anger lasts but a moment; God's favor a lifetime.
At dusk weeping comes for the night; but morning brings joy.
Complacent, I once said, "I shall never be shaken."
God of peace, you showed me favor; you made me
        like a strong mountain.
But when you hid your face I was struck with terror.
To you, God of peace, I cried out; I pleaded for mercy:
"What gain is there from my death, from my going down
        to the grave?
Does dust give you thanks or declare your faithfulness?
Hear, O God, have mercy on me; be my helper."

You changed my mourning into dancing;
you took off my sackcloth and clothed me with joy,
so that I may praise you and not be silent.
God of peace, I will give you thanks forever.

VI

God Will Protect You on Your Journey of Peace

THE HOPE OF THE PEACEMAKER

Those whose steps are guided by the God of peace,
whose way God approves,
may stumble, but will never fall,
for the God of peace holds their hand.

PSALM 37

The God of peace will keep you from all evil,
will always guard your life.
The God of peace will guard your coming and going
both now and forevermore.

PSALM 121

22 God Will Rescue You, God Will Deliver You, God Will Answer You
PSALM 91

Psalm 91 has been one of the key psalms of my life, since my earliest activist days. I well remember reciting it to myself, like a chant, as I faced my first arrest at the Pentagon in the early 1980s, as I slept in the cold in a refugee camp in the middle of the Salvadoran war zones in the mid-80s, as I languished in jail for my Plowshares action, as I walked through the streets of Belfast, where I lived in the late '90s, as I stood amid the seven-story "pile" of ruin that once was the World Trade Towers when I was the Red Cross Coordinator of chaplains in 2001, and on many other occasions. It has always been with me. The psalm itself, like the promise it holds, is a rock, a steady security worth holding on to. It says: God will rescue you, deliver you, answer you, be with you—no matter what. Good enough for me!

"No matter what happens to those around you," the psalm explains—plague, arrows, bombs, gunfire, warfare—"God will protect you." At some point, I said, "OK, God, I'll make a deal—I'll spend my life speaking out against war, violence, and nuclear weapons, and trusting in you and pointing to you, all the while trusting that you will protect me."

After all these decades, I can't say that God has ever let me down. Let me repeat that: God has never let me down. Despite all my foolishness in the art of public peacemaking, I have been protected. Go figure.

That leads to the second section: You shall not fear.

What? Fear's my best thing! That's impossible. We're all afraid.

"No! You shall not fear. Be not afraid!"

I remember, in my early twenties, studying Gandhi, reading that he had professed a vow of "fearlessness" in his thirties. I had to put the book down. Fearlessness? That's impossible. Gandhi himself was a terrified boy, if you read the fine print. OK, fine. Blah, blah, blah. I'll do it. If that's what he learned, after decades of struggle, I'll just cut to the chase and get with the program. Fearlessness—here I come. Fine. Let's try it.

A few years later, I found myself in the center of El Salvador's civil war, living in a jungle, building a refugee camp, not far from the Guasapa volcano, headquarters of the FMLN rebels, which was bombed on the hour every hour by the US Air Force. My sole job was to greet the death squads whenever they showed up. The thinking was that a blond-haired gringo—me—would not be killed and would send them scurrying off. And so, repeatedly, I was sent out to meet the death squads. There they were, surprisingly young, holding their US-made machine guns aimed right at me, demanding something or other. I would smile and offer them coffee; they would shake their heads and walk away. Once, as I talked to the young death squad member, I looked down at his machine gun and noticed a sticker he had put on it. It read, "Smile, Jesus loves you." I thought: God, you've got to be kidding me.

I could have been shot and killed on several occasions. I was right in the thick of it, one of the most violent places on earth, trying to be my best nonviolent self, even though few supported me. The war forced me to make some choices, but that was easy. I was surrounded by people of towering faith who had been inspired by Archbishop Romero, now Saint Romero, to trust in God.

In the middle of the night, sleeping on a cot, under a tin roof, in the middle of a war zone, I'd turn to God. Where was God? Would the Creator of the universe notice me, in the middle of a war, on the outskirts of the world? Could God protect me, and all of us here in the camp?

The answer was easy. A no-brainer. Of course! I would be fine! Even if I was killed, God would protect me. And so I did my job, made many friends, and felt a deep peace, hope, and joy that I had never known before or since. Strangely, it was the happiest experience of my life.

Over the years, in jail cells and police cars, in homeless shelters and soup kitchens, in the war zones of Colombia, Iraq, Afghanistan, Palestine, and Belfast, in Africa, India, Asia, and Latin America, those feelings of faith, hope, and trust have returned. I believed I was protected. Even later, in New Mexico, staring down the evil nuclear weapons labs, or facing hostile audiences or threatening police officers or violent demonstrations or even difficult relatives, I have felt quite secure in the protection of God. God said God would protect me, and that was good enough for me. I would take God at God's word, and never look back.

Forty years later, after a roller coaster life of war zones, jail, death threats, and church rejection, not to mention speaking to a million people, writing a pile of books and articles, and engaging with all kinds of people from all walks of life, I'm in the zone. I shall not fear. My life is in God's hands. I've surrendered into God. It's no longer me but God. When God wants to take me home to God, fine, I'll deal. It'll all be OK. No problem.

And so, we pray:

> *You who live in the shelter of the Most High,*
> *who abide in the shadow of the Almighty,*
> *say to the God of peace: "My refuge and fortress,*
>   *my God in whom I trust."*

> *God will rescue you from snare of the fowler,*
>   *from the destroying plague,*
> *will shelter you with God's pinions, and under God's wings*
>   *you may take refuge;*
> *God's faithfulness is a protecting shield.*
> *You shall not fear the terror of the night or the arrow that flies by day,*

nor the pestilence that roams in darkness, nor the plague
    that ravages at noon.

Though a thousand fall at your side, ten thousand
    at your right hand,
it will not come near you.
You need simply watch and see the punishment of the wicked.

It will not come near you. You need simply watch. That's the teaching. Around the world, people are hurting one another, oppressing one another, even killing one another, but if you follow my way of peace, love, and nonviolence, says the God of peace, you shall be safe. It's all about consequences: Those who live by the sword die by the sword. Those who live in peace and nonviolence will die in peace and nonviolence. Your task is to keep peaceful, faithful, contemplative, nonviolent watch. God will handle the rest.

Keep watch. That's the final commandment of Jesus, which he repeats over and over again toward the end of the synoptic gospels as the end draws near. "Keep watch," he tells his disciples. It's an invitation to remain awake, alert, contemplative, on the lookout. All hell is breaking out around you, but not within you. You will remain faithful to my way of nonviolence, and then you will see the presence of God in transforming nonviolent action, disarming the empire, saving humanity. Keep watch. It's still the key commandment of the gospels.

Note: the word "punishment" refers to consequences. If we engage in wicked activity, if we are violent, that wickedness, that violence will come back upon us. That's the punishment. So it's more like a warning: try to be as nonviolent, as gentle and loving as you can be, so that love and gentleness will come back upon you.

Because you have the God of peace for your refuge
and have made the Most High your stronghold,
no evil shall befall you, no scourge come near your tent.
For God commands the angels with regard to you, to guard you
  wherever you go.
On their hands they shall support you,
so that you will not strike your foot against a stone.
You can tread upon the asp and the viper, trample the lion and the
  serpent.
Because they love me, I will deliver them, says the God the peace;
because they know my name, I will protect them.
They will call upon me and I will answer;
I will be with them in distress;
I will rescue them and give them honor.
With length of days I will satisfy them, and fill them with my saving
  power.

The last five lines hold the key, the promise, the future. If we cling to God, we will be delivered. If we know God's name, we will be set on high. If we call upon God, God will answer. God will be with us and deliver us in our hour of need and give us honor, length of days, and the saving power of loving nonviolence. These are lines worth pursuing.

23 My Help Comes from the God of Peace ☀ PSALM 121

The invitation comes again in Psalm 121: place your hope, your help, your trust in the God of peace, the maker of heaven and earth. In these days of perpetual war, the 1 percent owning most everything, systemic racism and sexism, growing fascism, nuclear weapons, catastrophic climate change, billions in dire poverty, the extinction of millions of species—in these days, more than ever, we look to the God of peace for everything, every day, at every moment. This is the true path forward for all spiritual seekers.

Psalm 121 tells us clearly: the God of peace will take care of us:

I raise my eyes toward the mountains.
From whence will my help come?
My help comes from the God of peace, the maker
*   of heaven and earth.*
God will not allow your foot to slip; your guardian will not sleep.
Behold, the guardian of Israel never slumbers nor sleeps.
The God of peace is your guardian; the God of peace
*   is your shade*
at your right hand.
By day the sun will not strike you, nor the moon by night.
The God of peace will guard you from all evil;
the God of peace will guard your soul.
The God of peace will guard your coming and going
both now and forever.

God never slumbers or sleeps; God is a faithful guardian; God will guard your coming and going. Those are words worth testing.

How do we allow God to guard us and take care of us? Through daily prayer and meditation, where we give God at least once a day our full and formal attention, where we sit in quiet adoration and devotion to the God of peace, where we bring our concerns and questions of discernment. And more: through surrender.

The best way forward lies in the daily conscious surrender to God, morning, noon, and night. As a Christian, this means surrendering daily to the nonviolent Jesus. In other words, our mantra becomes,

"You take care of it." No matter what. Upcoming events that make us anxious, friends and relatives who are sick or suffering some kind of crisis, the latest daily horror—whatever. "You take care of it!" We're all getting older, all heading toward suffering and death. We won't have time in the end to focus ourselves on God; we'll be in too much pain. The wise take time now to practice trust in God, to surrender themselves to God, to practice letting God guard us, come what may. If we practice and get used to this mysterious reality, we'll be ready for that day when we surrender our hearts and lives eternally into God's hands. This is the journey that lies ahead, but it starts now.

And meanwhile, we get on with our daily task for justice, disarmament, peace, and the transformation of the world into a new culture of nonviolence. This is the will of the God of peace.

24 The God of Peace Is with Me to the End ☀ PSALM 138

Psalm 138 offers a positive affirmation to help us go forward in peace *with* the God of peace *to* the God of peace, knowing that our lives are in God's hands. We thank the God of peace at all times, as much as we can, no matter what, and we trust the God of peace as we do what we can for justice and disarmament, no matter how small or insignificant our efforts appear. We do what we can for a new world of peace. We do our little bit to help build a grassroots peace movement and to be peaceful with everyone. We serve those in need, advocate publicly for an end to violence, injustice, and war, teach nonviolence, and seek a more nonviolent world. Each day, we bow before God, praise God's name, thank God, and rest in the God of peace. Peace becomes our way of life. Peace is our life.

Psalm 138 sums up our basic attitude: gratitude, reverence, praise, and trust that you, God of peace, are with us for the rest of our lives. You, God of peace, will see us through, no matter what, even in the face of fascism, climate change, systemic injustice, insane violence, accident, illness, tragedy, and our own brokenness. So we say:

> I thank you, God of peace, with all my heart;
> I sing to you in the presence of the angels.
> I bow down toward your holy temple;
> I praise you for your mercy and faithfulness.
> For you have exalted your name and your promise.
> On the day I cried out, you answered me;
> you strengthened my spirit.
> All the kings of earth will praise you, God of peace,
> when they hear the words of your mouth.
> They will sing of the ways of the God of peace:
> "How great is the glory of the God of peace!"
> The God of peace is on high, but cares for the lowly
> and knows the haughty from afar.
> Though I walk in the midst of trouble,
> you guard my life against the rage of my enemies.
> You stretch out your hand; your right hand saves me.
> The God of peace is with me to the end.
> God of peace, your mercy endures forever.
> Never forsake the work of your hands!

The psalmist shares the experience of being answered by the God of peace. The God of peace answers, strengthens, and cares for the psalmist and all the lowly. The God of peace guards, saves, bestows mercy, and never forsakes the psalmist. Can we draw the same conclusion? Has God ever been personally mean to us? Has God ever personally hurt us? Has God ever condemned us? Anyone who spends time in quiet meditation over time knows that the answer to these questions is *no*. God only wants to love us, care for us, guide us, guard us, protect us, and lead us to God. The more we grow aware of this basic reality, the more we can let go of fear, surrender to God, and live in the loving protection of God.

Any nonviolent, loving parent would do anything to protect their child. A nonviolent loving parent dotes on the child, cares for the child, is there for the child, and never forsakes the child. That parent has pure, unconditional, nonviolent love for the child. Even if the child is crying or angry or yelling at the parent, the nonviolent loving parent has patience, compassion, and understanding to see through the fleeting emotion and still love unconditionally. That's the way God is with us at all times and for all eternity. God has pure, unconditional nonviolent love for each one of us. We don't realize this because we let our emotions, anxieties, fears, and cares get in the way of life in the Spirit of God. We are concerned about small petty matters and rarely take the long-haul, universal salvation point of view.

Yet at any moment we can turn back to the God of peace. As we trust more and more in the God of peace, we can surrender more and more to God and rest in the God of peace.

The nonviolent Jesus goes further to connect the dots and announces that everyone is the beloved son or daughter of the God of peace, and, therefore, everyone is called to be a peacemaker. I find this astonishing. We are peacemakers because we are the sons and daughters of God the peacemaker, sisters and brothers of Jesus the peacemaker. This is who we are. As peacemakers, we live in the peace of God; we trust God; we let God guard us and be with us. In that way, as we let go into the God of peace, we find our security in Peace itself, and our lives move from grace to grace, from peace to peace. When we die, we will be able to look back and see that the God of peace has always been with us, always been there for us, always affirmed us, always encouraged us, always tried to protect us. We will die grateful and at peace, surrendering ourselves to the God of peace, because we know the God of peace and know that we are safe in God's hands.

~~~

A word about gratitude: it is the key ingredient to this life of peace. A friend told me recently of her difficult years with cancer, including the tests, the chemo, the surgeries, the fatigue and illness. She realized from the start that the only way she could get through this suffering was with gratitude. So from day one she said over and over again to God, "Thank you for this cancer." From then on, she felt free. She kept thanking God, taking care of herself, and getting on with life as best she could. Eventually, they got the cancer, and she is now cancer free. And she remains grateful.

I had the same experience in jail. I felt infinitely grateful at all times, for anything and everything. I never felt so grateful to be alive. I had nothing, and yet I knew a deep gratitude and the peace that came with it. Now, years later, it's hard to get too down because life is so beautiful. There are always a million things to be grateful to God for, starting with the sun and the sky and the earth and the trees and the birds and the people who love us and the occasional miracles of peace. As we choose gratitude as a way of life, all the blessings of peace will be ours. And it's much more pleasant to go through our day-to-day lives feeling grateful and counting our blessings.

25 **Lead Me, Shepherd of Peace, into Green Pastures of Peace** ❋ PSALM 23

W alking along the ocean today by my home in California's central coast, I feel the cool breeze against me while the warm noon sun shines on me. White seagulls, egrets, cormorants, and swallows zoom by me, and the squirrels look up at me before scurrying over the cliff to their hideouts. As I walk along the cliff, a seagull comes gliding along, riding the thermal air wave. I can almost reach out and touch it. It does not flap its wings but looks around, at me, and then down at the sand for food. It's as if the gull is hanging from a string, or is actually a kite, but it is real and coasting along like me.

The sea is fairly calm. Up close near the rocks it's dark blue, then a dazzling cobalt, then turns to green, and on the horizon dark blue again. A boat or two sit on the distance, while up close, amid the rocks and breaking waves, a few seals poke their heads up and swim around. It's a California paradise of green mountains, ocean, beach, sky, and birds, and every time I walk these paths, I am at once strengthened, renewed, rejuvenated, reborn, and refocused.

This most famous of the psalms has comforted humanity down through the ages. If we let God shepherd us, if we surrender ourselves to the God of peace, we will be led to green pastures of peace. For us, the nonviolent Jesus is the Good Shepherd who leads us and guides us, and if we let him, he will keep us safe in peace.

Once, while living in Ireland, where the green hills are covered with sheep, I met a sheep herder who said sheep are the dumbest animals around. If so, then Jesus must have had a great sense of humor when he said, "My sheep know my voice and follow me when I call." Sheep never follow my voice, the Irish herder told me. Same with us Christians. Jesus is calling out to us but we ignore him and keep feeding on the grass.

I find that the minute I take my mind and eyes off the Good Shepherd, the minute I ignore his call, I lose my way. I wander off and get lost. I'm glad the Good Shepherd has his eye out for wayward sheep like me who are not that bright, because despite my best intentions, I end up alone in the hills or stuck in a bramble bush. He always comes looking for me and brings me back to the fold. I imagine Jesus carrying me back to the pasture while I complain the whole way. But once there, once I come to my senses, I'm grateful.

On other occasions, I think I've become a wolf in sheep's clothing, pretending to be a sheep. I have to repent of my selfishness and violence and let God disarm my inner wolf. I pray for the grace to reclaim my true inner sheep nature. In any case, the Good Shepherd is always there, trying gently to guide me, and asking me to help him shepherd others, too. Like many others, I find this psalm true—the God of peace has shepherded me through life, and though I have little money and few possessions, there is nothing I lack.

My favorite gospel text in recent years is Luke 10, where the nonviolent Jesus sends seventy-two disciples out ahead of him on his campaign of loving nonviolence. "I am sending you as sheep into the midst of wolves," he announces. In other words, we practice total nonviolence, even in the face of violence. The mission—to speak words of peace; expel the demons of war, racism, and nationalism; heal those wounded by the culture; and announce the good news that God's reign of nonviolence is at hand. I have tried to do this, and despite some hair-raising moments, I lacked nothing, and no harm came to me, as promised.

We're told the seventy-two disciples return rejoicing because people responded to their call. Jesus rejoices with them because they fulfilled his mission. He tells them that he has given them "power"—which I interpret to mean the power of nonviolence—that "no harm will come to you," and that their names are written in heaven. One could argue that it's the only occasion in the four gospels where Jesus is happy, and it's because his followers went out into the culture of violence as non-violent sheep into the midst of wolves.

〜

As we pursue a harmless life of peace and fulfill our gospel nonviolence mission, the Good Shepherd will guide our every step and Psalm 23 will be our everyday hymn. And so we pray:

> *The God of peace is my shepherd;*
> *there is nothing I lack.*
> *You let me graze in green pastures;*
> *you lead me to still waters;*
> *you restore my soul.*
> *You guide me along the right path for the sake of your name.*
> *Even when I walk through the valley of the shadow of death,*
> *I will fear no harm, for you are with me;*
> *your rod and your staff give me courage.*
> *You prepare a table before me as my enemies watch;*
> *You anoint my head with oil; my cup overflows.*
> *Indeed, only goodness and love will follow me*
> *all the days of my life;*
> *I will dwell in the house of the God of peace*
> *my whole life.*

As we recite Psalm 23, we live our way into it, and the words come true. We follow the nonviolent Jesus, our Good Shepherd, and become faithful sheep of nonviolence, living in peace, advocating peace, radiating his peace.

Over time, the words of the psalmist become our own: You let me graze in green pastures. You lead me to still waters. You restore my strength. You guide me on the right path. Even in the face of death, I will fear no harm. You are at my side. You give me courage. You set a table before me; you anoint me; you fill my wine glass. Indeed, only goodness, kindness, love, and mercy pursue me. I will live in the house of the God of peace from now on.

26 The God of Peace Has Been Very Good to Me ☀ PSALM 116

The other day I attended the memorial service for one of the great peacemakers of our time, Blase Bonpane. Blase died in April 2019, just before his ninetieth birthday. For five decades, he was the key peace and justice movement leader in Los Angeles, where he was revered and loved. Over 1,600 of us attended his memorial, which featured twenty-five speakers, including Rev. Jim Lawson, Dolores Huerta, Ron Kovic, and Martin Sheen, as well as singer Jackson Browne. One after another recounted the legendary works of peace Blase organized and mobilized—protests and solidarity projects especially for Central America. He affected the lives of thousands, maybe millions, and he did it, as everyone said, with joy and kindness. We were amazed as we reflected together on his full life. He always insisted that he was greatly blessed, that this was the holy work of God, and that the God of peace was behind all these efforts toward peace and justice.

It was such an inspiring occasion. Yes, we grieved, but we also rejoiced and left renewed to redouble our efforts for peace and justice, in light of the great activist's life.

Later, I thought that as peacemakers we probably don't realize the good impact we can have because we are so focused on the work of resistance to empire, injustice, and war. Only on such occasions as Blase's memorial do we grasp the impact of one another's lives, and the power and possibility of our own lives to make a positive difference. Only on such occasions do we see the finger of God working among us for positive social change. As we look back and recognize God's guiding presence in our work for justice and peace, we find new hope and energy to keep going, doing what we can.

As we walk the road to peace, as we try to be peacemakers and do our part for the nonviolent movements for justice, disarmament, and creation, it helps to stop and take stock of the journey and realize in our meditation how the God of peace has blessed us, protected us, guided us, and used us, and so, to give thanks with love to God. If we look deeply, we will find ourselves asking: How can we repay God for all that God has done for us? We try to keep faith and carry on.

Psalm 116 tells of someone who was suffering and persecuted, who cried out to God, and who was rescued and saved. It's a psalm of gratitude to God for protecting us, taking care of us, and guiding us. I think it's a psalm for us ordinary peacemakers.

> *I love the God of peace who listened to my voice*
> > *and my supplications,*
> *who turned an ear to me on the day I called.*
> *I was caught by the cords of death; the snares of Sheol had seized me;*
> *I felt distress and anguish.*
> *Then I called on the name of the God of peace, "O God of peace,*
> > *save my life!"*
>
> *Gracious is the God of peace, and righteous; our God is merciful.*
> *The God of peace protects the simple.*
>
> *God of peace, I was helpless, but you saved me.*
> *You have been very good to me.*

My soul has been freed from death,
my eyes from tears, my feet from stumbling.
I shall walk before the God of peace in the land of the living.

I kept my faith, even when I said, "I am greatly afflicted!"
I said in my alarm, "Everyone is a liar!"
How can I repay the God of peace for all the great good done for me?
I will lift up the cup of salvation and call on the name
    of the God of peace.
I will pay my vows to the God of peace in the presence
    of all God's people.

Precious in the eyes of the God of peace is the death
    of his devoted servant.
I am your servant, the child of your maidservant;
you have loosed my bonds. I will offer a sacrifice of praise
and call on the name of God.
I will pay my vows to the God of peace in the presence
    of all God's people,
in the courts of the house of the God of peace.

Several lines jump out that might be worthy of extra meditation:
I love the God of peace who listened to my voice and my supplications.
As we reflect on our journey to God, our prayer, our relationship with
God, we might ask, has God answered our cries, our pleas? If we ever
really asked God for help, I submit we probably were answered, and
the more we reflect on that experience of God in our lives, the more we
can open our hearts to love the God of peace. And that is the goal, that
is what God desires: our love for God. God has unconditional, nonviolent love for us. The more we accept it, enter it, and rejoice in it, the
more we might want to reciprocate with unconditional love for God.

God of peace, you have been very good to me. This is so helpful. It raises questions for all of us: Where is God in our life? Where do we experience the God of peace? When have we encountered God's presence, especially in our ordinary day-to day-life? Then this: has the God of peace been good to us? Has God ever yelled at us, terrorized us, or hurt us? Has God invited us into the Way of peace, and if we have accepted, where and when did we experience God's goodness? I love to ponder these questions. This is the definition of spiritual discernment: to ponder God's ongoing presence in our lives. This is why spiritual direction is so helpful—to have a coach with whom you can talk about your experience of God. Your spiritual director can point out what you don't see—that God has been good to you all along.

I shall walk before the God of peace in the land of the living. This is one of my favorite lines in the psalms. I want to live and walk in the land of the living, not the land of the dead, the land of violence, the land of war. I want to follow in God's wake; there I can be safe, happy, and at peace. "Walking" connotes mindfulness, movement, and discipleship. If we walk mindfully at peace, we are moving forward toward our goal, ultimately, toward God. We Christians want to walk in the footsteps of the nonviolent Jesus as his peacemaking disciples.

We might ask ourselves then: Are we walking in the presence of the God of peace in the land of the living? What part of us is still stuck in death and its metaphors? How can we be more fully alive and help others live life to the full together in the presence of the God of peace? When are we our best selves, whole and centered, in the fullness of life?

We want to choose the fullness of life and reject the ways of death. We want to walk in the land of the living. That is the path to our own happiness, and the hope and joy of God for humanity. It's in our own best interests to stop walking in the land of the dead. We want to get ready for resurrection so that we live with the living God and living humanity for eternity.

How can I repay the God of peace for all the great good done for me? Another key question. The God of peace has done everything for us— what can we do in return for God? Or to paraphrase St. Ignatius: What have we done for the God of peace? What are we doing for the God of peace? What are we going to do for the God of peace? These questions can be the driving force of our lives. Every day, we can thank God for what God has done for us and reflect on what we are going to do for God. That usually means getting out of ourselves, looking upon the whole world and all of humanity from God's perspective, and then trying to do something for justice, disarmament, and creation. The God of peace wants us to continue God's work for peace; so we try to carry on the holy work of peacemaking as an act of love and gratitude for the God of peace.

I will pay my vows to the God of peace in the presence of all God's people. With this statement, we pledge to remain faithful to the God of peace. We will walk in peace and nonviolence, be instruments of God's peace and nonviolence, and love God, all people, all creation, and ourselves for the rest of our lives. The saints and greatest peacemakers were notable precisely because they persevered with public peacemaking until the end of their lives.

That is what we want to do as well—to fulfill our vows of peace and nonviolence and stay on course with our peacemaking every day of our lives until our last breath. As we persevere on the journey of peace, we invite everyone we meet into God's life of peace so that peace spreads deep, far, and wide and our lives bear good fruit for the God of peace.

VII

Praise Be Peace

THE SONG OF THE PEACEMAKER

Shout joyfully to the God of peace all you lands;
worship the God of peace with gladness;
come before the God of peace with joyful song.
Know that God is the God of peace,
our maker to whom we belong, whose people we are,
God's well-tended flock.
Enter the temple gates with praise,
its courts with thanksgiving.
Give thanks to the God of peace, bless God's name;
good indeed is the God of peace,
whose love endures forever,
whose faithfulness lasts through every age.

PSALM 100

27 Let All the Earth Praise the God of Peace ☀ PSALM 148

Along of the coast of Northern Ireland, near the border, stand the towering granite Mourne Mountains. They look out over the sea and the miles of green fields, stone walls, sheep, and cottages. Along the edge of the mountains lies the entrance to the Silent Valley. It's five-mile walk passes a dam and a reservoir along a roaring river that winds through the mountains until it comes to a second massive dam.

I spent today walking with friends along the path by the river through the Silent Valley of the Mourne Mountains. I'm here leading a ten-day peace and nonviolence retreat in Northern Ireland with my friend Gareth. We've been offering presentations on peacemaking, meeting peacebuilders from all sides of the conflict, traveling along the coast, taking quiet time for rest and meditation, and sharing our own peacemaking journeys.

But for me, this was something new. I usually walk slowly, but my friends walk quickly. This felt good because we had many miles to go and I wanted to experience that brisk walk. We set off just as the sun came out, the first time in days. We walked into the wind with the towering granite mountains on either side of us, the fast-moving freshwater river down below on our left, the sheep scattered here and there stopping to stare at us, and above, massive white clouds that brought a mixture of light and shadow upon the mountains and distant green fields, as only they do in Ireland.

The walk through the Silent Valley and back was one of the great days. It was like stepping into another world, as if entering Tolkein's *Lord of the Rings*. In fact, C.S. Lewis walked these hills and paths throughout his youth and called this land his model for Narnia. It was a taste of heaven on earth and made me feel totally alive, one with Mother Earth.

It began to feel like Easter, like the first day of the New Creation, like all would be well if we only stopped and let Mother Earth speak to us. Notably, we walked in silence, because today was our silent retreat day. As I listened to Mother Earth, it seemed she was singing praise to the God of peace, and everything radiated peace.

~~

In October 2018, the Intergovernmental Panel on Climate Change released a devastating special report warning that we are moving toward irreversible climate chaos much faster than first thought, that humanity had better wake up fast and do everything possible to change its ways to prevent total global catastrophic climate change. The following May, another UN report announced that over one million plant and animal species faced immediate extinction unless humanity radically reversed its course and mounted a global campaign to protect creation. Millions of people have been taking to the streets around the world in recent years, and the movement for a global Green New Deal has been gaining traction, but still destructive polices continue, and the clock is ticking.

Extinction. Global Warming. Rising waters. Wild storms, hurricanes, droughts, fires, tornadoes, flooding. This is our new reality. The news of catastrophic climate change and the corporations and governments behind it leads to rock-bottom despair. What to do? We grieve, change our own lifestyles, take public action, and join the various environmental movements working for climate justice. Indeed, we need to do all these things.

But we can also develop a contemplative practice of nonviolence with Mother Earth. We can start walking gently with attentive mindfulness and appreciation of Mother Earth and all her plants and animals and with each step giving thanks and praise to the Creator and becoming one with Mother Earth and each other, the way we were originally created to be. Nonviolence and peaceableness are, therefore, the way forward.

Psalm 148 reads like an antidote to the turbulent times we are called to live in. It helps us be mindful, wise, gentle, nonviolent peacemakers, those who make peace with Mother Earth, all the creatures, all the people, all the universe, and with the Creator. Through this simple psalm, we become people who appreciate the wonders of creation and give thanks and praise to God for them. As we pray through this psalm and others like it, we find ourselves led out of despair into hope, out of darkness into light, out of our political numbness into nonviolent public action on behalf of Mother Earth and suffering humanity. We become, in other words, those who walk in the land of the living, peacemakers who make peace with one and all.

And so we pray:

Praise the God of peace from the heavens;
praise God in the heights.
Praise God, all God's angels; give praise, all you God's hosts.
Praise God, sun and moon,
Praise God, all you shining stars.
Praise God, you highest heavens, and you waters above the heavens.
Let them praise God's name;
for God commanded and they were created;
God established them forever,
God fixed an order that can never be changed.

Praise the God of peace from the earth,
you sea monsters and all the deeps of the sea;
fire and hail, snow and frost,
and stormy winds that fulfill God's command;
mountains and all hills,
fruit trees and all cedars!
Animals wild and tame,

creeping things and birds that fly;
kings of the earth and all peoples,
princes and all rulers!
Young men and women together,
old and young alike.
Let them all praise God's name,
for God's name alone is exalted,
God's majesty is above earth and heaven.
God has lifted high the horn of the people;
to the praise of all God's faithful.

Angels, sun, moon, stars, clouds, oceans, whales, sea creatures, fire, hail, snow, wind, mountains, hill, trees, animals, birds, and all people of every race, language, and way of life—all praise the God of peace. This is the meaning of life: to discover that we were made by a loving, gentle Creator to live at peace with one another, creation, and the Creator and then, one day, to enter the new Creation of God's eternal home to dwell face to face with the God of peace.

Nobody talks about this. Those who do often also support racism, sexism, war, executions, nuclear weapons—and climate chaos. They have no credibility. Nonetheless, the truth of creation and the nonviolence of the Creator stand before us, and we are invited into that truth, if we dare. When we die, we will regret that we wasted so much time contradicting the work of the Creator. Wisdom calls us to get with the program and undertake a new journey of peace with creation.

The deeper we step into peace, the more we find ourselves astonished by the God of peace. With every step of peace, mindfulness, and nonviolence, as we walk across Mother Earth, we open into gratitude. We give thanks to the Creator. Then, we start to praise the Creator. "Wow! You are so great! What you have done is so amazing! What you continue to do is so beautiful, so generous, so loving. We love you, we adore you, and we praise you. You alone are worthy of praise." Suddenly, the psalms make sense all over again.

Our peacemaking journey, quiet prayer, oneness with creation, and daily nonviolence toward all others lead us gently to praise the God of peace on behalf of and with all creation. This, we discover, is enough. We go forward, doing what we can to transform the culture of violence and destruction, but with every step, we also give thanks to the God of peace and offer praise. Because in the end, we know that with the God of peace, the Creator of all this beauty, all will eventually be well.

28 Praise God for the Grassroots Movements for Justice and Peace
PSALM 111

E very year around the Martin Luther King Jr. holiday, I spend a day or two rereading books about Dr. King and the Civil Rights Movement and watching documentaries about it. I do the same thing once or twice a year about Gandhi, studying his teachings on nonviolence, pondering his bold public efforts, wondering how I could likewise step up to the plate. Always, I give thanks to God and praise God for these historic peacemakers and their movements. I don't know where I'd be—where the world would be—without them. Their bold initiatives have now exploded into a permanent global grassroots movement of nonviolence.

Positive social change has only ever come about through bottom-up people power, grassroots movements of nonviolence, such as the early Christian movement, early monasticism, Franciscan peace movements, then the Abolitionists, the Suffragists, the labor movement, the antiwar movement, the antinuclear movement, through the women's movement, the environmental movement, the gay and lesbian movement, and the thousands of nonviolent movements for justice and liberation over the past century up until today. I see the finger of God in all these peaceful movements, the Spirit of God breathing new life into people, inspiring them to stand up, join the struggle, speak out, resist injustice, envision a new future, and be part of the nonviolent transformation of the world.

The grassroots movement to abolish Apartheid is one of the most inspiring examples. Led by iconic leaders—Nelson Mandela, Desmond Tutu, and Steve Biko—and many others, millions of people resisted the racist, white Apartheid regime and built a global boycott that eventually brought about elections, a new democracy, and Mandela as president. In the Philippines, hundreds of thousands of people were trained in nonviolence and took to the streets after the killing of Benigno Aquino, forcing the dictator Marcos to flee. In Liberia, Leymah Gbowee led tens of thousands of women to take nonviolent direct action, block the streets, and force the brutal dictator Taylor to flee.

These days, I thank the Parkland students who called for millions to march against gun violence and for gun control, the millions of students around the world who skipped school to call for climate justice, and the strategic developments of the International Campaign to Abolish Nuclear Weapons, the Nobel Peace Prize winners who led the UN to make a treaty to outlaw nuclear weapons. Over fifty nations have signed. And counting. Hundreds of thousands have marched recently in Hong Kong and Puerto Rico. People power is alive and well.

Billions of people are now involved in grassroots struggles for justice and peace. This has never happened before. This is what hope looks like. This, I believe, is the work of God. When I think of the social movements through history, I praise the God of peace and justice and feel renewed to join the struggle all over again.

That's the spirit I find in Psalm 111. Like Mary's Magnificat in the Gospel of Luke, Psalm 111 praises God for God's holy work among

God's people as God heals, liberates, disarms, and leads us to peace. So we say:

> *I will praise the God of peace with all my heart*
> *in the assembly of the upright.*
> *Great are the works of the God of peace,*
> *studied by all who delight in them.*
> *Full of honor and majesty is God's work,*
> *God's righteousness endures forever.*
> *God won renown for all these wondrous deeds;*
> *gracious and merciful is the God of peace.*
> *God gives food to those who fear God.*
> *God remembers the covenant forever.*
> *God showed powerful deeds to the people;*
> *God gave them the inheritance of the nations.*
> *The works of God's hands are true and just;*
> *all of God's decrees are trustworthy,*
> *established forever and ever,*
> *to be observed with truth and equity.*
> *God sent redemption to the people*
> *and decreed the covenant forever;*
> *holy and awesome is God's name.*
> *The fear of God is the beginning of wisdom;*
> *prudent are all who practice it.*
> *God's praise endures forever.*

I will praise the God of peace with all my heart. This is our new mantra. From now on we praise the God of peace with all our hearts. We love God, we bless God, we seek God, we surrender to God, and we worship God. This is the human journey of peace to the God of peace in a nutshell.

Great are the works of the God of peace. As we ponder the God of peace, the wonders of creation, and all the movements of peace throughout history and throughout the world today, we celebrate God's great work. We see God behind all that is good, all that leads to peace, all that heals humanity, all that welcomes God's reign of peace on earth.

Gracious and merciful is the God of peace. This is our lasting insight. God is not violent, not warlike, not deadly, not in any way like our violent, selfish selves. God is gracious and merciful, which means God is loving and kind, gentle and nonviolent, peaceful and peaceable. This is such good news, if we take the time to sit with it and imagine its implications. Not only are we personally in good hands, but so is the whole human race and all of creation. God is gracious and merciful. God will take care of us. God will lead us into a new more nonviolent world if we allow God.

And so we join God's movements for peace, disarmament, and justice and do our bit for a more peaceful world, and every step of the journey, we give thanks and praise.

29 Sing a New Song to the God of Peace
PSALMS 96, 98, 40

Today is a pristine, clear blue day with a brisk cool breeze that makes me feel fresh and alive as I walk along the cliffs above the ocean. The ocean, the sky, the birds, the sea creatures, the sand, the rocks, the green rolling hills behind me—they come alive, and I sense they are singing songs of peace to the God of peace.

I walk along the ocean; I watch the birds and sea creatures; I listen to the swallows dance through the air near my creek. I nurture peace and oneness with creation and find myself more at peace with the Creator. Surprisingly good days in an overwhelmingly bad time. Days of peace, in preparation for upcoming nonviolent resistance to the culture of war.

A few years ago, I got rid of TV. The bad news still lingers in the air, but I try to get as little of it as possible. I don't want to live in the despair of the poisonous air waves, to let the bad news rule my life. It's a struggle but well worth it. My friend the writer Anne Lamott calls this "radical self-care." My friend Fr. Cyprian, prior of New Camaldoli in Big Sur, goes further. This, he says, is the new asceticism.

I don't want to hear the culture's songs of war. I long to hear creation's songs of peace. And I do hear them, every day, sung by the ocean, the wind, the rivers, the mountains, the birds, the creatures, indeed all the earth. I feel the same exuberance as the psalmist in the great hymns of creation, 96, 98 and 40. Together, as here in Psalm 96, we sing to the God of peace:

> *Sing to the God of peace a new song;*
> *sing to the God of peace, all the earth.*
> *Sing to the God of peace, bless God's name;*
> *proclaim God's salvation from day to day.*
> *Tell God's glory among the nations;*
> *among all peoples, God's marvelous deeds.*
> *For great is the God of peace and greatly to be praised,*
> *to be revered above all gods.*
> *For the gods of the nations are idols,*
> *but the God of peace made the heavens.*
> *Honor and power go before the God of peace;*
> *strength and beauty are in God's holy place.*
>
> *Give to the God of peace, you families of nations,*
> *give to the God of peace glory and strength;*
> *give to the God of peace the glory due God's name!*
> *Bring gifts and enter God's courts;*

worship the God of peace, splendid in holiness.
Tremble before God all the earth;
declare among the nations: The God of peace is Ruler.
The world will surely stand fast and will never be shaken.
God rules the peoples with equity.

Let the heavens be glad; let the earth rejoice;
let the sea roar and what fills it resound;
let the fields be joyful and all that is in them.
Then let all the trees of the forest rejoice
before the God of peace who comes, who comes to govern the earth,
to govern the world with justice and the peoples with faithfulness.

The opening line touches me most: *Sing to the God of peace a new song.* No more tired songs of war, greed, selfishness, narcissism, ego, and fear. Try to sing something new, something grateful, something positive to the God of peace, a new song of peace, new songs of gratitude for creation, new songs of justice for the world's poor, new songs of disarmament. Psalm 98 continues the theme:

Sing a new song to the God of peace,
for God has done marvelous things.
God's right hand and holy arm have won the victory.
The God of peace has made God's victory known,
has revealed the triumph in the sight of the nations;
God has remembered love and faithfulness toward the house of
    Israel.
All the ends of the earth have seen the victory of our God.
Shout with joy to the God of peace all the earth;
break into joyous song; sing praise.

Sing praise to the God of peace with the lyre, with the lyre
  and melodious song.
With trumpets and the sound of the horn
shout with joy to the God of peace.
Let the sea roar and what fills it resound,
the world and those who dwell there.
Let the rivers clap their hands,
the mountains sing together for joy,
 before the God of peace who comes, who comes to govern the earth,
to govern the world with justice and the peoples with fairness.

The rock star Bono took up this challenge from the psalms and wrote a song based on Psalm 40 with the opening line, "I will sing, sing a new song." For many years, they ended their concerts singing this song, which they called "40." "I will sing, sing a new song," Bono would cry out, getting thousands to sing along with him. "How long to sing this song?" he would sing. "How long to sing this song?" He would lead the crowd in singing this chorus, and eventually he and the band would walk off stage. The crowd would continue singing and cheering and eventually leave with a whole new feeling of hope for their lives. I myself witnessed this new song in a vast assembly and, with twenty thousand fans, left rejoicing, exhilarated, and astonished.

U2's use of Psalm 40 was brilliant. They fulfilled the text by proclaiming God's good deeds to the vast assembly and literally "singing a new song to God." That's what we want to do, too—to sing a new song of hope despite the times and help others sing of the God of peace, no matter how bleak the world looks. Here's the psalm:

I wait for the God of peace
who bends down to me and hears my cry.
God draws me up from the pit of destruction,

out of the muddy clay,
and sets my feet upon rock.
God steadies my steps
and puts a new song in my mouth, a hymn to God.
Many shall look on in fear
and they shall trust in the God of peace.
Blessed are they who set their security in the God of peace,
who turns not to the arrogant
or to those who stray after false gods.

You, yes you, O God, my God, have done many wondrous deeds!
And in your plans for us there is none to equal you.
If I wished to declare or tell them,
there are too many to recount.
Sacrifice and offering you do not want;
you opened my ears.
Holocaust and sin-offering you do not request;
so I said, "See; in the scroll of the book it is written of me.
I delight to do your will, my God;
your law is within my heart!"

When I sing of your justice in a great assembly,
see, I do not restrain my lips,
as you, God, know.
I have not hidden your saving help within my heart;
I speak of your loyalty and your salvation.
I do not hide your mercy or faithfulness from a great assembly.
God of peace, may you not withhold your compassion from me.
May your mercy and your faithfulness continually protect me.

With Bono and the psalmist, we too promise to sing of God's justice and peace, not to restrain our voices, not to hide God's mercy or faithfulness, to speak of God's loyalty and salvation. This is the mission—to sing a new song to the vast assembly, as best we can, to praise the God of peace and invite everyone everywhere to join the chorus.

VIII

Love and Truth Will Embrace; Justice and Peace Will Kiss

THE VISION OF THE PEACEMAKER

God of peace, your love reaches to heaven,
your faithfulness, to the clouds.
Your justice is like the highest mountains;
your judgments, like the mighty deep;
all living creatures you save, God of peace.
How precious is your love, O God!
We take refuge in the shadow of your wings.
Continue your kindness toward your friends,
your just defense of the honest heart.

PSALM 36

The God of peace does righteous deeds,
and brings justice to all the oppressed.
Merciful and gracious is the God of peace,
slow to anger, abounding in love.
As the heavens tower over the earth,
so God's love towers over us.
As far as the east is from the west,
so far have our sins been removed from us.
The kindness of the God of peace is forever,
toward the faithful from age to age.

PSALM 103

30 **Bless the God of Peace, My Soul**
PSALM 103

I 'm walking down a narrow, cobblestoned street in Assisi, Italy, during a break in the Pace e Bene Pilgrimage of Peace and Nonviolence. It's been an amazing, uplifting, consoling experience. Thirty-five of us have formed a close community of peace. My friend Ken Butigan offers brilliant presentations on Francis and Clare in the mornings, while I later preside at Mass at one of the holy sites. The weather has been perfect—cool and brisk in the morning, sunny and hot in the afternoons, cool again in the evenings. It's Francis and Clare all the time, peace and nonviolence all the time. We all feel like we've entered the promised land, the Cloud of Unknowing, some kind of liminal space of peace—dare I say it?—the reign of God on earth.

But that is precisely why we came—to learn the lessons of peace and nonviolence from Francis, Clare, Jesus, and one another, to taste God's reign of peace, to see if we could walk in the promised land of peace, to practice gospel nonviolence, to be renewed to carry on our work as peacemakers. Here in Assisi, it all sounds doable. It's consolation upon consolation.

Not that Francis and Clare had it easy. Their lives were a constant struggle with rejection, poverty, suffering love, setbacks, failures; opposition from the church, relatives, and rulers; and betrayals from within their communities. But they kept their focus on the peacemaking Christ and practiced peace, nonviolence, and mindfulness full-time, and their lives have born tremendous fruit. Because of them, Assisi has become the model city of peace, a city set on a hill that gives light and hope to millions.

As I walk these streets, I'm immersed in the life and story of the great peacemaker—here is where Francis was baptized as a baby long ago; here is the mayor's house where he publicly renounced his family and wealth and walked outside the city with Lady Poverty; here are the caves where he and his early companions retreated in prayer and solitude; here is the place where he was laid on the ground and died; here is his tomb, way down below the basilica, where crowds of people come every single day to bow, kneel, pay their respects, and pray.

In this liminal space, I ponder the life of our greatest saint and, like the other pilgrims, take a second look at my own life and the path before me, the things I'd like to do for peace and the God of peace before I die. I long to go deeper into peace and nonviolence and live in the Holy Spirit of this peace pilgrimage for the rest of my life. I want to root my work for peace, like Francis and Clare, in my relationship with the God of peace. In other words, I want to focus myself morning, noon, and night on the God of peace, that everything I do and say may be for the God of peace. Is that possible? Can we become as immersed in the God of peace as the saints, so that the God of peace lives and works among us?

I walk the streets of Assisi, taking it all in, breathing in the Spirit of peace, communing with nature and friends, pondering the eternal questions, and surrendering myself all over again to the God of peace. With each step, I give thanks and rejoice and turn to the God of peace. I have brought the psalms with me on this pilgrimage of peace, and for the first time in a long while feel their consolation. Today, walking the hills of Assisi, a psalm like Psalm 103 comes naturally:

> Bless the God of peace, my soul; all my being, bless God's holy name!
> Bless the God of peace, my soul; and do not forget all God's gifts,
> who forgives all your sins, and heals all your diseases,
> who redeems your life from the pit
> and crowns you with love and mercy,
> who fills your days with good things
> so your youth is renewed like the eagle's.

The God of peace does righteous deeds and brings justice
  to all the oppressed.
God made known God's ways to Moses, and all the Israelites.
Merciful and gracious is the God of peace, slow to anger, abounding
  in mercy.
God will not always accuse and will not stay angry forever;
God has not dealt with us according to our sins, nor requited us
  as our wrongs deserve.
For as the heavens tower over the earth, so God's mercy towers over
  those who fear God.
As far as the east is from the west, so far has God removed
  our sins from us.

As a father has compassion on his children,
so the God of peace has compassion on those who fear God.
For God knows how we are formed, remembers that we are dust.
As for humanity, our days are like the grass;
we blossom like a flower of the field.
A wind sweeps over it and it is gone, and its place knows
  it no more.

But the mercy of the God of peace is from age to age,
  toward those who fear God.
God's salvation is for the children's children of those
  who keep the covenant,
and remember to carry out its precepts.
The throne of the God of peace is set in heaven;
God's dominion extends over all.

Bless the God of peace, all you angels, mighty in strength,
  acting on God's word,

obedient to the divine command.
Bless the God of peace, all you hosts, all you ministers
  who carry out God's will.
Bless the God of peace, all you creatures,
  everywhere in God's domain.
Bless the God of peace, my soul!

St. Francis teaches us to live in relationship with the God of peace, to remember our small place in the grand scheme of things, to see the limitations of our lives, to trust in the compassion of God and radiate that same divine compassion to everyone, to be as nonviolent as the God of peace and to bless the God of peace with every step we take. And so we go forward on our pilgrimage of peace and nonviolence, blessing God, blessing all the creatures, blessing all our sisters and brothers, and living in the blessing of God.

31 The God of Peace Is Gracious and Merciful ✸ PSALM 145

S t. Francis casts such a large shadow that St. Clare can easily get overlooked, but we do well to learn her story because she, too, is one of the greatest saints in history. One of Francis' first followers, she risked it all to leave her wealthy family, join his community, form her own monastic order of women, and settle into a life of prayer in San Damiano. She, too, was a towering peacemaker. Once she stopped an impending invasion of Assisi by walking out to greet the invading soldiers with the Blessed Sacrament. They were so shocked that they fled in terror, and the war never happened. Clare lived to be sixty. When she died, she left a shining example of peace, prayer, and voluntary poverty. She became widely revered as the epitome of the Christian peacemaker.

Once during our pilgrimage, we gathered for Mass at the tomb of St. Clare, down in the crypt of the basilica. We sang hymns, offered prayers, and read from the Gospel of Luke the story of Mary's calling. We were focusing on the lessons of women peacemakers, so I reflected on Mary as Jesus' teacher of nonviolence. In Mary's story, Luke outlines three spiritual movements of nonviolence, as I write in my book *Mary of Nazareth, Prophet of Peace*: the Annunciation as contemplative nonviolence, which leads to the Visitation as active nonviolence, which leads to the Magnificat as prophetic nonviolence. Clare lived this lifelong pilgrimage of nonviolence, and we prayed for the grace to do likewise.

So many psalms exemplify the positive, grateful, joyful spirit of St. Clare. One that fits her spirit is Psalm 145, which blesses God for God's gentleness and goodness. I can imagine it being a text close to Mary and Clare:

I will praise you, my God; I will bless your name forever and ever.
Every day I will bless you, and praise your name forever and ever.

Great is the God of peace and greatly to be praised,
whose grandeur is beyond understanding.
One generation praises your deeds to the next
and proclaims your mighty works.
They speak of the splendor of your majestic glory and
tell of your wonderful deeds.
They speak of the power of your awesome acts
and recount your marvelous deeds.
They celebrate your abounding goodness
and joyfully sing of your justice.

You, God of peace, are gracious and merciful,
slow to anger and abounding in mercy.

You, God of peace, are good to all,
compassionate toward all your works.
All your works give you thanks, God of peace,
and your faithful bless you.
They speak of the glory of your reign
and tell of your mighty works,
making known to all your mighty acts,
the majestic glory of your rule.
Your reign is a reign for all ages,
your dominion endures for all generations.

The words of the God of peace are all trustworthy;
 God's works are all loving.
The God of peace supports all who are falling and raises up
 all who are bowed down.
The eyes of all look hopefully to the God of peace,
who gives them their food in due season.
You open wide your hand and satisfy the desire of every living thing.
God of peace, you are just in all your ways, merciful in all your works.
You, God of peace, are near to all who call upon you,
to all who call upon you in truth.
You fulfill the desire of those who fear you;
you hear their cry and save them.
You watch over all who love you ... .
My mouth will speak the praises of the God of peace;
all flesh will bless God's holy name forever and ever.

St. Clare, like Mary, was focused on God at all times. She centered herself in the presence of the God of peace and lived in contemplative, mindful peace. She reached out in loving service to the poor and needy through her active nonviolence. And she spoke out against war in her prophetic nonviolence. She wanted to follow Jesus on the path of peace and love. Great saints like her teach us to live the wisdom of devotion and praise for the God of peace, as Psalm 145 suggests, so that we too might follow the nonviolent Jesus on the path of peace and love, come what may.

This became a familiar theme during our pilgrimage of peace and nonviolence. Where are we on the journey of discipleship to the nonviolent Jesus? How focused are we, like Francis and Clare, on the God of peace? What new, risky, public steps can we take to help stop war, love our enemies, bring about justice, and reconcile people, as Francis and Clare did?

During our afternoon breaks, I often met with some of the pilgrims for individual sessions and encouraged them to keep their eyes on the nonviolent Jesus, to ask Jesus to guide them on their journey, and to try to live as servants of the God of peace. One pilgrim, Michele, a secular Franciscan, told me that she felt called to take another step forward on her journey of public peacemaking but didn't know what to do next. I encouraged her to take her desire to Jesus, and put it before him. Everything else, I suggested, would fall into place.

Upon her return to the States, she connected with a group of Franciscans and learned that the following week there would be a national Catholic day of action at the US Capitol, where people would speak out against the US mistreatment of immigrants at the border and protest the detention of immigrant children. Some people even intended to kneel down in the main Senate office buildings and risk arrest.

Michele had never done nonviolent civil disobedience before, but she took it to prayer, and the next thing she knew she was being hauled off in handcuffs. She took a public stand against the US persecution of immigrants and children, which touched everyone in our circle. Here's what she wrote afterward:

Staying within my comfort zone was becoming untenable. My work on the Middle East still seemed important but insufficient; what was

I doing about peace, human rights, and social justice right here in the United States? Yes, I prayed, voted, supported peace organizations doing good work, and kept informed about the issues, but I increasingly felt I should do something more—especially as a professed member of the Secular Franciscan Order. Our Rule is bracing on this point: "Let them individually and collectively be in the forefront in promoting justice by the testimony of their human lives and their courageous initiatives. Especially in the field of public life, they should make definite choices in harmony with their faith."

In the summer of 2018, an invitation arrived about an upcoming pilgrimage to Assisi from an organization called Pace e Bene, with the express aim of connecting Franciscan values and spirituality to a life of active nonviolence.

The trip in June 2019 was like a week in heaven: visits to the major sites in the lives of St. Francis and St. Clare, daily Mass with invigorating homilies by Rev. John Dear, lectures by Ken Butigan bringing out the revolutionary social and peacemaking initiatives of the two saints, deep conversations with fellow pilgrims who had varied experiences in spirituality and activism—and all while surrounded by the matchless beauty of the medieval city of Assisi and Umbrian countryside. I came away feeling encouraged and inspired, accompanied on the journey by new friends.

Just a few days after my return from Assisi, I was invited to the protest. I suspected the time for action had come. Still, I was nervous. Would a protest against the detention of immigrant children really do any good? Would I be glad or sorry at the end of the day that I participated? I prayed for guidance over several days.

After participating in a webinar for potential participants, some of my fears were allayed. The protest seemed well planned, and the organizers presented a clear theory of change: we would do civil disobedience to show that some Catholics were willing to take risks to speak out for immigrant children—and hopefully to inspire more Catholics to speak up as well. The organizers were clear about what would happen at the protest, what the risks were for those who would be arrested, and what the police processing would involve. They told us to bring a photo ID, $50 to pay the likely misdemeanor fine, a Metro card to get home—and not much else.

Organizers and protestors gathered early at a church near the Capitol to meet in person and go over the details. Asked for a show of hands, a large number said we were doing civil disobedience for the first time.

After the press conference on the lawn, we headed into the Russell building and found the rotunda. We donned signs with photos of children who had died in detention and formed a large circle, with several participants lying down to form a cross in the center. After a blessing by a priest, we chanted a few slogans and started praying a Rosary. Almost immediately the police interrupted with a warning to disperse. By the third warning, those who were not willing to be arrested had left. When I saw Sister Marie being led off in handcuffs, I knew it was getting real. The police were courteous, with many looking uncomfortable arresting nuns in veils, priests in Roman collars, Franciscan friars in brown robes, and laypeople praying the Hail Mary.

Nothing quite prepared me for the disempowered feeling of having my wrists zip tied behind my back. There followed several hours of police processing: transport to a police station, pat-downs, belongings put into plastic bags, sitting on folding chairs in a large, semi-open room that was very warm but made tolerable with fans and bottled water. My fellow detainees did not complain but provided cheerful encouragement and interesting conversation—particularly the large contingent of Sisters of Mercy. As each detainee finished the paperwork, paid the fine, and was released, the remaining cheered and applauded, while even the police officers grinned at our good cheer. Outside the station, protest organizers were waiting to offer water, snacks, rides, and thanks. I rode the Metro home with one of the other seventy people arrested, and we were surprised to discover that we were fellow parishioners.

I arrived home, where my husband promptly ordered my favorite pizza and listened to the story of the day. While I had feared he would disapprove of my participating in civil disobedience, he told me he respected what I had done.

As I relaxed in the evening, I recalled that during my Assisi pilgrimage I had asked Pace e Bene nonviolence training coordinator Veronica Pelicaric how I could discern whether to undertake greater activism. She quoted to me Civil Rights leader Howard Thurman: "Don't ask what the world needs. Ask what makes you come alive, and go do it."

The Catholic Day of Action left me perspired, exhausted, and hungry, but did it make me come alive? Yes indeed it did. (Published in *Franciscan Action*, July 2019)

> *God of peace, you are good to all, compassionate toward*
> *   all your works.*
> *God of peace, you are trustworthy in all your words,*
> *   and loving in all your works.*
> *You support all who are falling and raise up all*
> *   who are bowed down.*
> *You are just in all your ways, merciful in all your works.*
> *God of peace, you are near to all who call upon you, to all*
> *   who call upon you in truth.*
> *You watch over all who love you.....*
> *My mouth will speak the praises of the God of peace;*
> *all flesh will bless God's holy name forever and ever.*

As peacemakers, we can encourage each other to take new steps forward on the pilgrimage of nonviolence, just as Mary and Clare did. We can get over our initial fears, let the God of peace guide us, and discover that the God of peace is trustworthy and near to us. We can take another step on our pilgrimage of peace and nonviolence, take some public action for justice and peace, and take heart, trusting that the God of peace is drawing us all together into God's reign of peace.

32 The God of Peace Will Proclaim Peace to God's People ☀ PSALM 85

The key holy site in the St. Francis story stands down the hill from Assisi in what was once a remote forest far outside the safety of the city gates. It's the Porziuncola, a little handmade chapel that St. Francis himself built stone upon stone. This was the heart of his pilgrimage, the place where he returned throughout his life, the place where he founded his community, the place where Clare joined his community, the center where the community gathered every few years for their first assemblies, and the place where Francis returned to die. It still stands today, but now with the massive Basilica of St. Mary of the Angels that surrounds and contains it. There it is just before the altar, a little chapel dwarfed by the glorious basilica.

It is the end of our weeklong pilgrimage. We have been granted a special privilege—to celebrate Mass in the Porziuncola. We crammed in together to sing hymns of praise, offer prayers of peace, and hear once again the mission to be sent out as peacemakers. We read from Luke 10, how Jesus sent out the seventy-two disciples on the mission of peace and nonviolence, to be "like lambs in the midst of wolves," to offer greetings of peace, to heal the sick, and to proclaim God's reign of peace on earth. We received communion and left the Porziuncola singing, ready to go forth as peacemakers into the world of war. It was a highlight of our experience.

Here in this little chapel, long ago, Francis saw a vision of Jesus and Mary. They asked what he wanted most of all, and he asked that every human being be allowed into heaven. And Jesus said OK. Later the pope granted Francis' wish that once a year, on the August anniversary of that apparition, anyone who visited the chapel and received the sacrament of reconciliation would be granted eternal life. Needless to say, it is a special place, holy ground indeed.

~

While most Franciscan pilgrimages recite the names, dates, and historical details, we tried to do something new: to focus on St. Francis' message of peace and nonviolence, to challenge ourselves to live up to this great gospel calling. It took us all to a much deeper level, into that liminal space that Francis knew, where we experienced the God of peace alive and well, giving us the gift of peace and sending us forth to proclaim God's peace to the whole world.

Of all the psalms, the one most focused on the message of peace is Psalm 85. There we are presented with a promise of peace beyond our imagining—a poetic vision of love, truth, justice, and God's own peace that is coming. It's the kind of vision and promise one experiences in the Porziuncola. It's a psalm worth taking to heart for the rest of one's life. After pointing out how God will let go of anger and forgive us our faults, the psalmist celebrates God's peace and call to peace:

> I will listen for the word of the God of peace.
> Surely the God of peace will proclaim peace to God's people,
> to the faithful, to those who trust in the God of peace.....
> Love and truth will embrace;
> justice and peace will kiss.
> Truth will spring from the ground;
> justice will look down from heaven.

Psalm 85 is one of the most beautiful prayers, one of the most imaginative poems, one of the greatest pieces of writing in all of literature. Better than Shakespeare, Yeats, and Eliot rolled into one. It combines our best prayer for God's mercy upon humanity, our best hope for God's word of peace, our best vision of what that peace might look like.

I think this psalm is the hope and vision of the nonviolent Jesus. He dreams this dream and acts on it. In his Sermon on the Mount, he teaches us how to make this hope and vision come true. His prayer fulfills Psalm 85: *Your reign of peace, your will of justice, be done on earth as it is in heaven.*

The text instructs us in the basics of prayer, and in doing so, gives us a way forward. All we have to do is listen attentively every day in our contemplative prayer for the word of the God of peace, and then act on that word. If we do, good things will follow.

That means we sit in silent meditation and ask the God of peace to speak, wait for God to speak, hear exactly what God has to say, and try to fulfill that word. This is the journey of the peacemaker. This is what we will be doing in heaven, so meditation is actually just practice for the new life of peace to come.

When we listen, we will hear the God of peace speak of peace. We will immediately feel more peaceful and set about to speak of peace and work for peace. The psalm urges us to build our lives around that word of the God of peace. We let God give us peace and say peaceful, loving words to us, and we thank God for this kindness. Next, we go forward and speak that word of peace to others. We teach that word of peace and help each other unpack that word of peace. And we try to create the conditions where that word can take root, bear good fruit, and eventually come to a new harvest of peace.

Psalm 85 calls us to live and breathe God's holy word of peace. It presumes we want to be the people who are faithful to the God of peace. As people who trust the God of peace, we spend our energies heralding a new world of peace without war, injustice, poverty, violence, killing, or nuclear weapons, and promoting a new world of nonviolence.

~~~

I've often wondered what this poem means. What does it mean to say love and truth will embrace, justice and peace will kiss? How does truth spring up from the ground and justice look down from heaven? These are poetic images, Zen koans, well worth pondering.

We can all name the countless ways that hatred and untruth have embraced, that injustice and war have kissed, the myriad times when lies have sprung up and injustice looked down on us. But it's harder to imagine love, truth, justice, and peace coming together like some cosmic breakthrough. I think this beautiful, poetic image makes sense only if we are attentively listening to the word of peace from the God of peace and if we are trying to be the God of peace's faithful peacemakers.

Psalm 85 makes me think of Coretta Scott King, whom I admired and knew slightly. I remember her description of the March on Washington on August 28, 1963, when Dr. King announced his famous dream of reconciliation. She wrote after his death that the sight of hundreds of thousands of people standing before them at the Lincoln Memorial was the most extraordinary experience of her life. For a brief moment, she wrote, that sea of smiling, hopeful black and white faces revealed to her the reign of God here on earth.

Every now and then we perceive moments when love and truth embrace, when justice and peace kiss, when the fruit of our lifelong peace work suddenly becomes a harvest of peace: the joyful fall of the Berlin wall; the release of Nelson Mandela from prison, and his election as president of South Africa; the People Power movement in the Philippines; the hammering of nuclear weapons in a plowshares action; the victory of Leymah Gbowee in Liberia; the abolition of the death penalty or the end of a war; and so forth. These historic moments fulfill Psalm 85.

Psalm 85 invites us to attend to the word of the God of peace, to hear that word of peace, to base our lives on that peace, to speak only that word of peace, and to do our small part to help make real that great unforeseeable, unimaginable moment when love and truth embrace and justice and peace kiss.

~~~

If you go back and read Psalm 85, it does not start that way. I've jumped ahead to the good part. It begins as a lament. It pleads with God to relent, to forgive us, to let go of anger because of our rejection of God's way of love and peace, and to give us the gift of life once again. It begs God to save us from our own violent self-destruction.

Once, God of peace, you favored your land, restored your faithful people's fortune, forgave their guilt, pardoned all sins, withdrew your wrath, and turned away from anger, the psalmist writes. "Restore us once more, God our savior....Please give us life again, that your people may rejoice in you. Show us, God of peace, your steadfast love; grant us your salvation."

Scholars say the psalm evokes the prophetic voices of the postexilic period, around the fifth century BCE. In other words, it was written in the same hopeless, violent, imperial context we suffer through today. In light of our wars, weapons, greed, racism, massacres, and environmental destruction, we too need to cry out to the God of peace to have mercy on us and help us reclaim the wisdom and sanity of peace and nonviolence.

Psalm 85 leads to a whole new kind of prayer, a prayer not just for ourselves individually but for all humanity:

God of peace: we don't deserve it, but give us your peace anyway. We've rejected your gift of nonviolence, but give us your gift of nonviolence anyway. We've renounced Jesus' Sermon on the Mount, but teach us to live by its principles and practices anyway. Give us the gift of your reign of peace on earth.

End our wars in Afghanistan, Iraq, Palestine, Yemen, and Pakistan. Help us to dismantle our nuclear weapons and weapons of mass destruction. Help us to close the Pentagon, Los Alamos, and all our military bases and to invest instead in nonviolent methods of conflict resolution. Help us to feed the hungry, heal the sick, and abolish poverty so that the causes of war are eradicated and everyone can live in dignity with equal justice, that we might welcome your reign of peace here on earth. Make us once again your faithful people, your holy peacemakers. Let us see love and truth embrace, justice and peace kiss. Let us welcome your reign of peace here on earth.

If we can return to the God of peace, and pray for God's gift of peace for the whole human race, like Coretta Scott King and the psalmist, we might be given the vision of truth and love embracing, justice and peace kissing. But we have to lament our wars and violence. We have to take up God's way of nonviolence. We have to beg the God of peace for the gift of peace. We have to listen attentively each day for the holy word of peace from the God of peace.

Only then might we be ready for those breakthrough moments when love, truth, justice, and peace meet in joyful celebration. That day is worth pursuing, every day for the rest of our lives, for on that great day, we will see God face to face and know the fullness of peace.

CONCLUSION

It's a Tuesday morning, nearly a year after I started these musings, and I'm driving up Route 1 again along the California Coast back to the Camaldolese Monastery on the mountaintop in Big Sur.

It's a cool, sunny day, and the sea is a mixture of green and blue. Pelicans, gulls, and egrets fly along the shore while the waves crash upon the rocks down below. The road twists and turns but I feel calm and peaceful as I take in the glory of God's backyard.

The treacherous two-mile road up the mountain was rebuilt over the summer. They cut through a different part of the mountain and paved a whole new, much safer road. I drive slowly, up and up, until I arrive at the top. I park by the gift shop, walk into the church, and sit down. The silence enfolds me, holds me, embraces me. It's like deep-sea diving. Suddenly, you are in another realm. Within moments, I'm "content with the grace of God," as St. Romuald urged long ago.

After a while, the noon vigils begin. "God, come to my assistance," one of the monks begins. "Lord, make haste to help me," we respond. We open our prayer booklets and start to chant the psalms together. Today it's 123, 124, and 119:

To you I raise my eyes, to you enthroned in heaven.
Like the eyes of a servant, so our eyes are on the God of peace,
till we are shown mercy. **123:1–2**

Our help is in the name of the God of peace,
the maker of heaven and earth. **124:8**

Blessed are those whose way is blameless, who walk by the teaching
of the God of peace. Blessed are those who observe God's decrees,
who seek the God of peace with all their heart. They do no wrong;
they walk in God's ways. I will praise you with sincere heart. **119:1–8**

A closing prayer is offered, and we receive the final blessing. I linger in the silent church, soaking up the peace and quiet. Once again, I'm astonished at the tangible peace of this mountaintop sanctuary. Once again, I ponder our common call to be peacemakers, to live in this peace as the beloved sons and daughters of the God of peace, to share this peace with everyone and all creation.

The psalms offer clues about how to fulfill our peacemaking vocations: have nothing to do with violence or war; renounce the idols of death; seek peace and pursue it; practice steadfast nonviolence; serve the poor, do justice, and resist systemic injustice; honor Mother Earth and her creatures as you honor all sisters and brothers, all people everywhere. Live in the wisdom, grace, and light of peace.

Most of all, trust in the God of peace. Make the God of peace your one secure refuge. Live for God, seek God, serve God, wait for God, and love God. Let God be your all in all, so that you forget yourself and turn into the peace and love of God. Discover God's graciousness, kindness, and compassion, and start to mirror that same generosity toward everyone else. Know that God is the God of peace, and proclaim this revelation in the vast assembly.

Here in the monastery, in the silence of the church, with the psalms still hovering in the air, I enter the peace of God and feel the presence of the God of peace. I remember again that God is peace, that the nonviolent Jesus is the embodiment of peace, and that his Holy Spirit is infinite peace. I recall that peace is the fruit that comes from the daily practice of universal love and total nonviolence, which means it's a gift: Jesus' resurrection gift, our birthright, our promised land, our inheritance, ours for the asking.

I whisper softly, "Thank you, God of peace. Bless you, God of peace. May we all welcome your gift of peace. May we all seek your reign of peace. May we all serve your reign of peace.

"May your reign of peace come at last upon the earth. Open wide our hearts to abolish war, weapons, and violence forever, to create a new culture of nonviolence here on earth, to let truth and love, justice and peace, hope and history rhyme anew. Disarm and awaken our hearts that we may protect Mother Earth and all her creatures, that we might make justice and disarmament a reality, that we might know you as our true refuge, our rock, our fortress, and our God.

"Lead us to sing a new song: *Praise be the God of peace. Praise be the peace of God. Praise be peace.* Amen."

QUESTIONS FOR PERSONAL REFLECTION AND SMALL-GROUP DISCUSSION

1. Which psalms touch you and inspire you the most? What phrases, lines, words speak to you? As you recite your favorite psalms, what happens to you, how are your transformed, how are you led once again to God? How do the psalms lead you deeper in faith toward God?

2. What do the psalms teach you about God? How does the perspective of gospel nonviolence transform your reading of the psalms? Where do you experience the God of peace in your life, and how do the psalms confirm your experience of a loving, nonviolent God?

3. How do you react to the antiwar psalms, to the teachings that God stops wars; that God does not support the weapons of war; that the God of peace does not want us to rely on weapons of war, on the idols of death, but on God alone? How can we live this message of peace more and more?

4. How do the psalms that celebrate the glories of creation and the Creator inspire you? How does reading and praying through the psalms of creation, in light of catastrophic climate change, help you, rebuild your confidence, and lead you to new hope in God? As you pray through those psalms focused on the wonders of creation, how are you inspired to change your life to live in greater nonviolence toward Mother Earth, her creatures, and all people? How do the psalms help you appreciate the glories of nature more and more, as God's gift to you? What new steps can you take to support the global grassroots peace and environmental movements?

5. What does the teaching that "God is our refuge" mean for you? How do you take refuge in God? What other things do you take refuge in, and how can you begin to place your refuge more and more in God alone? How do you trust in God, despite the world's violence and your own brokenness and the inevitability of suffering and death?

6. Many psalms cry out in lamentation to God for help and mercy. How do these psalms touch you, inspire you, help you? In particular, how does Psalm 22, the cry of despair and its movement to hope in God, affect you at this point in your life? How does this psalm help you understand the paschal mystery of Jesus?

7. Many psalms insist that the God of peace will protect you and defend you. How have you felt God's protection in your life? How do you place your ultimate security in God? What does that mean for you? How has God rescued you, answered you, delivered you, saved you?

8. Where do you see the finger of God throughout history? How do you see God at work in the world today, disarming us, guiding us, and leading us to a more just, more peaceful world?

9. How do you praise God? How does creation praise God? What new song are you going to sing to the God of peace? How is authentic, sincere praise of God connected to integrity of heart, the practice of nonviolence, concern for the poor and the earth, and trust in God, not in weapons?

10. What does the teaching, "Love and truth will embrace, justice and peace will kiss," mean to you? How is God bringing peace to the world these days, in your own life and globally? How does call God us to be peacemakers these days?

11. What does it mean for you to be a peacemaker? How do the psalms, which inspired Jesus, inspire you to be a peacemaker, a person of faith, hope, love, and nonviolence?